Praise for

This book is an opportunity for district administrators and staff to glean strategies and ideas that improve performance in their schools. The validity comes from data presented through the lens of someone who's been there. I applaud Mr. Carter's effort to make a difference in the delivery of education today.

—**Dr. Keith M. Bell Sr.**, instructional facilitator, The Ohio State Student Leadership Collaborative

Authentic, practical, and actionable! Dwight Carter gifts us stories and lessons that empower us to be purpose-driven in leadership and in life. These principles equip us with the attitudes and actions we need to nurture relationships and cultivate a positive culture with appreciation, awareness, clarity, and intention. If you are ready to silence your inner critic and be GREAT, this book is for you!

—**Lainie Rowell**, author of *Evolving with Gratitude*

In *Be GREAT,* Dwight Carter reminds us why we became educators. His voice is a quiet, strong reminder that we should make the most of our opportunities to help others in these tough education times. This book is a must-read for anyone wanting to reflect, grow more robust, and be more effective.

—**Mark White**, author, consultant, and former superintendent

Dwight is a phenomenal educator, so the practical and inspiring content in *Be GREAT* is no surprise. Educational leaders like Dwight continue to push the boundaries of what it means to be an educator, understanding that when we build authentic and reciprocal student-teacher relationships, we build community. For us, the greatest testament to Dwight and the influence of his work is our occasional farewell remark to each other as we leave for work in the morning: "Be great!"

—**Kenyona Nicole Walker, PhD,** and **Todd Anthony Walker, JD, PhD**

While many of us strive to be great, the reality is that we typically settle on being good or even average. Through personal stories and professional experiences, seasoned leader Dwight Carter lays out a path to greatness that anyone can follow.

—**Eric Sheninger**, best-selling author and keynote speaker

Dwight focuses on challenging the status quo of education and what happens in a school building. This book empowers the reader to look at school culture via five principles. It is not just for the leader of a learning environment but for all educators. #BeGREAT!

—**Dr. Marcus Belin**, 2021 NASSP Digital Principal of the Year

I met Dwight years ago at a Jostens Renaissance Global Conference and immediately knew he was someone I needed in my professional network and as a personal mentor and friend. Lucky for me, over the years, he has become exactly that. In my years of knowing Dwight, "be great" has been his mantra, signature, and daily reminder. But it isn't just some saying he uses to gain followers in the education space. Being great is truly who Dwight is at his core. After reading this book, you, too, will see that genuine spirit within him.

—**Dr. Tara Campbell**, educator

In addition to sharing his own stories and those of other educators, he also shares relevant quotes, research, and questions for reflection and discussion. Learning from other educators and having specific questions to reflect on make this book an excellent choice. It is a well-written book that will help educators reflect on and grow in their practice.

—**Julie Diaz**, partner, N2 Learning

This book would be an excellent book study for any school staff or even a book club out of school. You will be lifted by Dwight's honest, heartfelt observations and the wisdom he has gained as a highly successful, award-winning educational leader. Thank you, Dwight, for delivering this to us!

—**Dr. Steve Woolf**, founder and director of Wild Heart Teacher

Dwight Carter's newest book invites and inspires educators into a new paradigm for school. Clear guideposts, compelling stories, and the receipts to back it all up make this book one of the most noteworthy releases of the year. This isn't just a book; it's a gift to anyone who's ever aspired to "be great" but struggled to do this consistently amid the messiness and complexity of life.

—**Brad Gustafson**, author and Minnesota Principal of the Year

BE GREAT

DWIGHT L. CARTER

BE GREAT

Five
Principles
to Improve
School Culture
from the Inside Out

This book is available at special discounts when purchased in quantity for educational purposes or for use as premiums, promotions, or fundraisers. For inquiries and details, contact the publisher at books@impressbooks.org.

Published by IMPress, a division of Dave Burgess Consulting, Inc.
IMPressbooks.org
DaveBurgessConsulting.com
San Diego, CA

Paperback ISBN: 978-1-948334-56-3
Hardcover ISBN: 978-1-948334-61-7
Ebook ISBN: 978-1-948334-57-0

Cover and interior design by Liz Schreiter
Edited and produced by Reading List Editorial
ReadingListEditorial.com

I dedicate this book to students, staff, colleagues, and family, past and present, who have touched my life. Hopefully, I have touched your life, too. Be GREAT!

CONTENTS

Foreword 1

Introduction 4

ONE: What We Control 9

TWO: Be Grateful 26

THREE: Be Relational 50

FOUR: Be Enthusiastic 77

FIVE: Be Authentic 102

SIX: Be Teachable 126

Conclusion 144

Notes 150

Acknowledgments 156

About the Author 157

More from IMPress 158

FOREWORD

One of my favorite quotes is from a blog, *Marc and Angel Hack Life*: "Being positive does not mean ignoring the negative. Being positive means overcoming the negative. There is a big difference between the two."

Keep that in mind for a second.

Dwight Carter and I met over a decade ago on Twitter when we were both administrators looking to find better opportunities for our schools. The interesting thing about Twitter in those days is that there were a lot of teachers on the platform and very few principals. In fact, administrators were so few on the platform that it was an amazing place to complain about your administrator because they probably couldn't figure out how to get on social media anyway. But Dwight and I were there, and I was so glad that I met him.

One Saturday afternoon, Dwight sent me a private message, and even though we had never talked, he asked if I had time to connect with him. As if we had never known a time when we weren't in each other's lives, I asked him for his phone number and called him, and it was like we were picking up right where we'd left off in a previous conversation.

We talked about some things that were happening in his school and in mine that we were struggling with, and how we could figure out a way forward to best help our communities. We also learned about each other on a more personal level, and we have been close friends ever since. Even though we have known each other for less than a quarter of my life, I can't remember a time when I wasn't able to pick up the phone and call Dwight for advice or to chat about our families in a very real and authentic way. I look up to him not only as an educator but as a friend and a dad.

So when we talked about publishing this book, I was excited, because I couldn't think of a better example of someone who finds innovative ways to move forward for his community and himself than Dwight. As I read through the book, I was surprised that I was surprised by how Dwight not only shares amazing insights into teaching, learning, and leadership, he also shares many of the struggles he has had in the process. But I have never known Dwight to not be his authentic self or to not share the tough moments in his life, in and out of school. I then realized that he is the epitome of the quote I love so much: "Being positive does not mean ignoring the negative. Being positive means overcoming the negative. There is a big difference between the two."

That is what you will read in this book.

You will read the stories of downs with the ups. And we need that authenticity more than ever. What Dwight shares made me reflect on how I have been in some of those same situations. But even through those dark moments, Dwight finds a way to shine a beautiful and illuminated path forward.

It reminded me that great storytellers have a gift. Not only do they share their stories, they have a way of placing the reader in the middle of them. Dwight does that throughout this story, which makes it even more powerful, because his journey is so relatable.

I don't want to ruin the story, but here is one quote from the book where Dwight's vulnerability really impacted my thoughts as I read: "I handled it wrong. It was completely out of character, and in hindsight, that event was a culmination of a few years of frustrating experiences. My attitude impacted my actions that day. I lost my temper and violated the trust others had in me."

Can you honestly say that in your years of education you have never had a moment like this one? I know I have, and the realness of

Dwight's statement made me feel that I was not alone. This profession can wear on us and bring out some of our worst moments.

But it can also bring out our best.

And Dwight will remind you that it is not that we don't have those tough moments, because we all do, but that we can find a way through to something better than what we had before.

Being GREAT is first and foremost about wanting to be better for yourself, but as Dwight shares throughout, it is about making those around you better as well.

You are about to walk hand-in-hand with an incredible leader. I could not imagine not having him as a part of my professional and personal life. As Dwight reminds us, being GREAT is not an endpoint but a journey we commit to that makes us better each day.

Thank you for being a part of this journey for yourself and those you serve.

—George Couros

INTRODUCTION

Principles are fundamental truths that serve as the foundation for behavior that gets you what you want out of life. They can be applied again and again in similar situations to help you achieve your goals.

—Ray Dalio

I first submitted my proposal for this book to George and Paige Couros in July 2019. They were excited and eager to read more about what it means to Be GREAT. Paige replied right away, and as I read her response, I felt overwhelmed and defeated by the story I was telling myself: "No one wants or needs to hear from you."

So the proposal and brief synopsis sat in my Google Drive, and I sat . . . stuck. I'd facilitated workshops and presentations on what it means to Be GREAT for years. Each time I walked away on a dopamine high thanks to the participants' responses and follow-up emails. However, no one knew that what lay beneath the surface of my high was the feeling of being an impostor. Have you ever felt that way?

Periodically, I'd give George a call, and each time he'd ask, "How's the book coming along?" I'd share some lousy excuse about all the other things I had going on in my life. In reality, a recent job change meant I was less busy than I had ever been. I'd make some false promise about how I was going to get moving on the book. George would offer an enthusiastic "Get it done!" before we ended our conversation. In my head, I wanted it, but in my heart, I knew I wouldn't be any closer to writing this book the next day, the next month, or the following year. I lied to him, and I lied to myself. "Impostor," I told myself.

In March 2020, the COVID-19 pandemic hit us hard and ultimately disrupted our world. Schools closed, and the nation was on lockdown, requiring us to stay home. Many people resorted to creative outlets such as writing, painting, new forms of physical fitness, etc. Writing this book loomed over my head even more because I had nothing but time. It wasn't until Saturday, August 8, that I came to grips with what my barrier was: I was afraid!

To Be GREAT requires a change in attitude, and this will guide one's actions. I know it, I teach it, I present about it, I encourage others to do it, and I don't always live it. Because of this last fact, I was afraid to write this book. How could I put to paper what it means to Be GREAT and encourage others to Be GREAT themselves? I was afraid of being a hypocrite and an impostor.

The Be GREAT principles are guideposts that I strive to live by every day. But the reality is that I still struggle to live a life of gratitude, especially during challenging times. To catch my breath or escape, I choose to isolate myself from the most important relationships in my life. When my ego gets in the way, I don't live in my purpose with the passion and enthusiasm it takes to positively change lives and impact futures. There are times when I may be resistant to sound advice or learning something new, which is the opposite of what it means to be teachable.

Yet you are reading this introduction because being GREAT is not about being perfect. It's about being *consistent*, *persistent*, and *resilient*.

What Does It Mean to Be GREAT?

By the time I became a head principal in 2005, email was an important tool to share information. I wanted to inspire and influence the behaviors of those who received my emails, so I thought about what words I could use as a sign-off besides "Sincerely" or "Yours Truly." There is nothing wrong with those choices; I just wanted something more.

As I was driving to school one day, two words popped into my head: "be great." I immediately got excited. I thought it was a simple, empowering message. So I started using "Be Great" as my sign-off on all correspondence, including emails, newsletters to staff and parents, and every letter I sent from school. However, after about a month, I thought it was a bit cheesy, so I stopped using it. A few staff members noticed the change and asked why. They said it inspired them to think differently about their day. They wondered if I had gotten into trouble or was told to stop using it, which was hilarious to me!

I explained that I thought it was a bit cheesy. They assured me that the message was, in fact, the opposite. It was a friendly reminder to them to give their best, and it was an inspiration. I also heard from some parents who said they'd started using the same sign-off at work and received positive feedback. I was shocked, but I started using it again and did so for the remainder of the school year. I still use it to this day, and I also use the hashtag #BeGREAT on my daily inspirational Twitter and Facebook posts. It now has a much deeper meaning.

About eleven years ago, I became much more intentional about my personal and professional growth. I embraced the influence I had and took it more seriously as I settled into my role as a school leader. I asked myself, "What does Be GREAT actually mean to you and why?" I reflected on my life and my experiences as a student, teacher, coach, and principal. I thought about all the relationships I had established with students, other educators, and families in the community I served. I thought about my successes, failures, opportunities, and setbacks. I thought deeply about my core values and whether my attitude (my settled way of thinking and feeling) aligned with the beliefs that guided my behavior and actions. It was no easy task, but I began a journey that has led to more appreciation, awareness, clarity, and intentionality in my life. I reflected upon the following questions:

- How do I want to be remembered?
- How can I best serve others throughout my day?
- When do I have a more positive attitude and experience the most joy throughout my day?
- What has led me to this point in my life?
- What can I do to be a better person?

It was through this process that my Be GREAT principles were formed. When applied consistently and intentionally, they will improve your attitude and actions in every area of your life.

- **Be Grateful.** Express your appreciation of the kindness you receive from others. Also, appreciate the tangible and intangible blessings each day, including family, a supportive network of friends and colleagues, and opportunities disguised as problems.

- **Be Relational.** Identify and develop the skills to create, grow, and maintain positive connections with others. Recognize those who have inspired you, mentored you, and shared words of encouragement and constructive criticism to help you grow.

- **Be Enthusiastic.** The Greek root of *enthusiasm* is *entheos*, meaning *divine inspiration*. Therefore, to be enthusiastic is to understand our purpose and align our core values so that our purpose is clear.

- **Be Authentic.** Learn about yourself, including your character strengths, triggers, weaknesses, boundaries, and aspirations, so that your head and heart are aligned.

- **Be Teachable.** Have a desire to learn by being taught. Be willing to receive constructive criticism and correction, be humble enough to seek new knowledge, be ready to develop and strengthen personal skills, and be coachable.

Each principle has its own chapter, and each chapter begins with an inspirational quote that sets the stage for the strategies described. Each chapter also includes stories from inspirational educators who describe how their work embodies the Be GREAT principles. Finally, each chapter concludes with a summary and three questions for conversation that will encourage you to reflect on your learning. You may answer these questions independently or with a colleague.

This book is not a how-to guide or self-help program. I hope to challenge, empower, equip, and inspire you to understand how much control you have over your life, your choices, your attitude, and your actions. You can impact the culture in your school or classroom. Educators are under immense pressure, and in the age of constant, high-speed change, this pressure is not going to decrease. It's only going to increase. Therefore, we must find ways to respond more effectively to change and develop skills to navigate through the challenges that lie ahead. I hope that these stories and strategies encourage you to keep moving forward in a direction aligned with your core principles. Let's get started!

ONE

WHAT WE CONTROL

If you don't like something, change it. If you can't change it, change your attitude.

—Maya Angelou

There's not much that's worse than a person with a consistently bad attitude. They drain energy from the room and can be exhausting. I like the quote above by Maya Angelou because it's so simple and empowering. The only things we have absolute control over are our attitude and actions. These two things alone have the most significant impact on our lives. But what does attitude mean? Before I define it, let me tell you a story that I'm not proud of.

I was sitting in my office on a nice spring day when a staff member came to my door and announced that some students were riding scooters in the hallway. Since it was late spring and the latter part of the school year, "senior prank" was my first thought. I asked where this was happening and how many students were involved, and I quickly got out of my chair and walked to the lobby with the staff member. I saw three other staff members waiting by the lobby door. When I approached them, I asked, "Did you say anything to the students?" They replied, "No, we came to let you know." For some reason, that irritated me, and I got angry. Not visibly angry, but it was just beneath the surface.

I left them at the lobby door and went to search for the scooter riders. As I scanned the area, I envisioned a large group of seniors racing their scooters down the long hallway while onlookers livestreamed the proceedings. I imagined the comments and the aftermath. The more I thought about it, the worse my attitude got. Then I noticed something. The hallways were quiet—extremely quiet. How could scooter races in a school hallway be quiet?

I continued searching with my walkie-talkie in hand. I walked upstairs, turned the corner, and came upon two students. One was carrying a scooter, and the other was casually riding along. My anger reached its peak. I grabbed the scooters, said some things I'm too embarrassed to write, and told the young men to leave because they had already completed their senior exams and their classes were over. I was still scanning the hallways when I got a message on my walkie that said two seniors were riding skateboards just outside the back entrance. I headed that way and got to the doors just as the young ladies in question walked in. I went off on them! We'd had problems with them for most of the year, so I was done with their shenanigans. I took one of the skateboards and told them to get out of the building. Like the two young men, these seniors' school year was over. The only thing left was the commencement.

I stormed back toward my office, and at the lobby doors, I saw the four staff members huddled together. I walked past them with the scooters and skateboard in hand, and the look on my face told them not to say a word. One opened the office lobby door for me, and my anger came to a boil. Acting completely out of character and irritated to no end, I took two steps, dropped one of the scooters and the skateboard, and threw one of the scooters at the wall! I was shocked, they were shocked . . .

I picked the scooter up, noticed the damage to the wall, and immediately felt like a complete idiot. My secretary ran out of her office, yelling, "Dwight, you can't do that! You can't do that!"

My attitude shaped how I handled the scooter situation. I handled it wrong. It was completely out of character, and in hindsight, that event was a culmination of a few years of frustrating experiences. My attitude impacted my actions that day. I lost my temper and violated the trust others had in me. I immediately called my superintendent, apologized to the staff members and my secretary, and called the students' parents. I had the opportunity to apologize to the students at our senior walk event. They accepted my apology, but the damage was done. Coincidentally, my car was egged in my driveway about a week later. I found out years afterward that the two young ladies with the skateboards were responsible. They even invited me to their graduation party. That's savage!

According to the *New Oxford American Dictionary, attitude* means a settled way of thinking or feeling about someone or something, typically reflected in a person's behavior. It's like grooves in a trail. Attitude demonstrates a level of comfort, ease, and familiarity. It also reflects that one's way of thinking, feelings, and behavior have developed over time. Suppose we are not aware of or lack a specific set of skills? We might quickly settle into an attitude that makes it difficult to overcome challenges or adjust to the slightest of changes. When we have a bad attitude, we have trouble recognizing the difference between an inconvenience and a crisis.

How Your Attitude Impacts Your Actions

When I became principal at New Albany High School in 2014, I learned a valuable lesson about the importance of attitudes and actions. We faced a $7.5 million deficit, which required the passage of an $8.9 million levy, or we would have to make massive staff and program cuts. The news was devastating to the staff and community.

Unfortunately, the levy failed, so we had to make some significant changes to how we did business. We had to eliminate nearly one hundred positions from every area. We lost staff from our curriculum department, assistant principals from three of the four buildings, custodians, bus drivers, teachers, secretaries, and educational assistants. Our pay-to-participate fees also increased, which created a burden on families.

It was an emotionally and physically draining process to have to reduce staff. Inevitably, there was a loss of security, fear and anxiety increased, and educators felt less valued. Isolation increased while collaboration and a desire to do anything "extra" seemed burdensome. Our attitudes and actions had a major influence on the short-term and long-term outcomes for staff as we tried to help them navigate through these tough times.

We could not change the outcome of the levy, so we focused on how we communicated with others. During times of uncertainty, the people we serve need to hear a clear and concise message. No fluffy, vague, or ambiguous talk is acceptable because it only increases doubt, a lack of trust, and anxiety. This approach may entail making decisions that are not going to be popular, but this is part of communicating specific and concrete information.

We chose to reexamine our vision by asking reflective questions about where we wanted our school to go and what we wanted it to become. It was challenging because we were experiencing loss and an overwhelming sense of uncertainty.

Leading through loss forces us to think creatively about how to do business with less, which is not always a bad thing. A part of the process requires us to identify constraints and challenge ourselves and others, and we must share ideas about how to do business in a different, more productive manner.

We broke through the barrier of isolation by becoming more intentional about collaboration. We created a plan of action and communicated it to small groups at first. Then we reshaped and reviewed our plan before sharing it with a broader audience. We sought input from others before making a decision or relying on others to make a decision. Having some level of collaboration is important. Make sure you have an operational definition of collaboration before moving forward. If not, you can cause more harm than good.

Leadership takes courage, especially through tough times. Not only did we have to control our attitudes and actions—we also had to influence those of everyone else in the building. People suffered from survivor's remorse, class sizes increased, and there were lingering hard feelings about how badly the levy failed. It was a roller coaster ride of emotion for most of the year, and it extended into year two. In the spring, we were able to gain some traction when we added a few teacher and administrator positions.

Year three started off strong! We hired a dynamic team of administrators, including a new athletic director from out of state named Richie Wildenhaus. His impact was immediate. He focused on two things: bringing more clarity to our pay-to-participate program and developing our coaches. Richie partnered with a leadership coach named Jack Slavinski. Our coaches loved Jack's style, approach, and processes to get positive results. He soon began working with our student-athlete leaders. Jack and I became friends after a few conversations, and I hired him to work with our building leadership team because we were not making the progress I thought we should be and kept facing internal conflicts.

Our building leadership team consisted of administrators and department leaders. During a meeting one day, Jack asked a few questions and listened intently for about forty-five minutes. I turned to him and asked, "Jack, what are your thoughts?" He smiled and said, "I notice the levy keeps coming up as the reason why you are not able to move forward with some initiatives. How long ago was that?" A few of us glanced around the room, and one of the leaders said, "Two years ago." Jack smiled. Then, quite frankly and sincerely, he asked, "How long are you going to drag that anchor?" The room went silent.

It was a simple yet profound question. The implication was that our lack of progress was due to our unwillingness or inability to own our problems and move forward. We'd become victims of an event, and our choice to use the levy as our anchor hindered our ability to see that we had other options. Our default behavior was to blame others, complain about our circumstances, and resist new ideas. Our narrative, attitude, and actions were controlled by the anchor we refused to pull up.

Here's a question: What anchors are you dragging around?

During disruptive times like those we are currently facing, we hold on to emotional anchors. If we lack emotional intelligence, these anchors can be detrimental to our school culture and climate. According to author and editor Thomas Oppong, "Emotions influence our attitudes and judgments, which in turn, influence the decisions we make. Your success and progress largely depend on your ability to understand and interpret how you feel before making any snap judgment."[1]

Education is one of the most noble professions. Our primary responsibility is to provide a safe learning environment that enables students to develop cognitive and social skills and find their pathway to success. Because we're always working with people, education is also a highly emotional profession. It can take a toll on us if we lack the proper attitude to handle the ever-increasing expectations placed upon us.

NBA legend and Naismith Memorial Basketball Hall of Famer Maurice Cheeks illustrates how one's attitude dictates one's actions. After retiring from the Philadelphia 76ers, Cheeks was an assistant coach for several NBA teams before he became the head coach for the Portland Trail Blazers. A thirteen-year-old girl named Natalie Gilbert won a singing contest and was selected to sing the national anthem during a nationally televised Portland Trail Blazers basketball game. Natalie was not just talented; she also diligently practiced for her performance.

On April 25, 2003, in front of thousands of cheering spectators, two basketball teams, referees, head coaches, assistant coaches, and millions of fans watching on TV, the announcer introduced Natalie. After polite applause, the announcer asked everyone in the arena to stand for the singing of the national anthem. Natalie stepped onto the court just ten or so feet away from the referees and began to confidently sing, "Oh say can you see by the dawn's early light. What so proudly we hailed at the twilight's last gleaming." And then she faltered: "The stars that … the stars … that …"

Panicked, she stumbled over the words again. Then she quickly looked around, wide-eyed and scared, searching the crowd for someone, anyone, to help her. Coach Cheeks glided to her side and gently said, "C'mon." He put his left arm around her shoulder, leaned into her, and began singing the words with her. After a few more lines, Natalie regained her confidence and bellowed out the remainder of the song. Coach Cheeks gestured to the crowd to join in, and suddenly every person in the arena was singing the national anthem. Amid raucous applause from the crowd, Natalie looked up at Coach Cheeks and mouthed, "Thank you!" She leaned into his chest, and he embraced her one last time before rejoining his team at the bench.

When Cheeks was being inducted into the Hall of Fame, he was asked about this experience. He said, "I heard the national anthem so many times, so I had to know the words. … I just looked and I knew she was struggling. I am a father. Everyone can understand that. Once

I saw it, I did not want her to be standing in the middle of all those people and not know the words. So I just kind of reacted. I don't even know why."[2]

His attitude, or settled way of thinking and feeling, led him to respond to the situation at hand, which influenced many others' behavior. Out of the people close to Natalie, only one person decided to act, and that was Coach Cheeks. He saw a young person in need, ignored his ego, and sang along with her even though he could not carry a tune! He also influenced thousands of fans to sing loudly along with her. Coach Cheeks rose to his level of training. How can we apply what he did to our own lives? Here are some points to consider:

- He was empathetic—not sympathetic—to the problem. He felt *with* Natalie instead of feeling sorry *for* her. He saw that she was in a hole and provided a ladder so she could climb out of it.
- He set his ego aside. He chose to act even though he is not a singer. He sang along with Natalie to support her in her journey.
- He encouraged others to join in. He showed Natalie she was not alone in her struggle.
- He didn't force others to join in. He modeled the way and gestured encouragingly to get others to sing along.
- He celebrated Natalie, not himself, when it was over. He showed us how important it is to celebrate our students as they make progress toward their goals and meet the standards they set for themselves.

How many times have you created a Maurice Cheeks moment by responding to a student or colleague in need? How many times have you experienced a Natalie Gilbert moment and needed someone to provide a lifeline? We have opportunities every day to choose our attitude. However, in our glamorization of busyness, we tend to let our to-do lists dictate our days, attitude, and mindset. Our mindset determines how we respond to life. Our attitude determines how we engage and interact with others. Unfortunately, our feelings often hijack our mindset based on our lived experiences, a barrage of negative messages, and negative emotions. We must intentionally develop the emotional intelligence to respond appropriately to the myriad challenges we face daily.

Our default behaviors become ingrained in us over the years, and regardless of the outcome, we rely on these behaviors to navigate through life. By learning to respond appropriately despite our feelings, we will become better at meeting challenges in a way that positively influences others. But first, we must silence the inner critic who is ready to talk us into relying on our default behavior.

Jack Slavinski

Professor, Leadership Coach, and Consultant
Lead4Influence (jackslavinski.com)
Columbus, Ohio

Jack Slavinski, a leadership coach and consultant with Lead4Influence in Columbus, Ohio, can break down complex concepts about leadership development, cognitive training, and mindset into usable strategies that make a difference. He came into my life at a pivotal moment. As we got to know each other, we realized we were aligned in our approach to leadership and life. Jack reminds us that our influence increases when we develop the proper mindset to lead ourselves and others.

Mindset is everything. People use the word loosely without explaining or fully understanding its meaning and personal power. Mindset is about our beliefs, values, attitudes, and behaviors. Committing (mindset) to managing one's self-talk (thoughts) is essential to being effective in life. So is emotional intelligence (self-awareness, emotional management, and social awareness).

Mindset establishes the beliefs and attitudes that inform how we approach situations. When we are more positive and open to adapting and persevering, we grow and achieve more. Think about it: it's difficult to be negative or stuck in a certain way of thinking and to be open or adaptable to new views or people at the same time. Mindset starts with knowing one's beliefs, as it's those beliefs that ultimately lead to developing the right behaviors. Staying positive, managing self-talk, reflecting on our behaviors, committing to self-awareness, and being willing to question our beliefs (call it a belief inventory) are all essential to keeping an effective mindset. Everyone on our planet gets stuck or feels negative. It's a matter of being self-aware, understanding why it's occurring, learning from it, and getting our brain back into a positive "I can do this or need to do this" state.

A person who believes they can't change—because of the way they were raised or because that's just who they are—or who is deficient in self-awareness or emotional regulation will experience challenges. We all set the tone for our day. We have far more control over how we respond to each day's situations than we give ourselves credit for. Setting one's mindset is a top priority every day.

To help educators overcome the stressors of life, I have them develop a diverse network of relationships with individuals they respect, trust, and can speak with candidly on a regular basis. I remind them not to go one-dimensional and focus solely on their job. They should have other outlets that fuel meaning and purpose. Tracking progress is essential, so I tell them to keep a journal of all the good moments. This helps balance their positive/negative ratio. I also advise them to invest time in learning true resilience-building skills and strategies. There is a lot more to this than mindfulness and yoga.

What You Say to Yourself Matters

The words we speak to ourselves significantly impact our attitude and actions. For example, you may be the type of person who makes a daily to-do list to help you accomplish essential tasks. You may write your list on a Post-it, on your phone, or in a notepad. Whatever you use, the to-do list has become a staple productivity hack.

When I facilitate a professional development session, I ask participants to review their lists and put "I have to" or "I need to" in front of each item. Once they do that, I ask them to describe how they feel about their lists, and the replies are typically the same:

- Anxious
- Full of dread
- Overwhelmed
- Frustrated
- Exhausted
- Stuck
- Afraid
- Nervous

Occasionally, someone will say they feel excited or happy about their list, but it's an anomaly. When I ask participants why they feel the way they do, the responses boil down to the same thing every time: they feel controlled or held hostage by the tasks because they are things that "have to" be done.

After a few minutes of discussion, I ask them to look at their lists again and replace the words "I have to" or "I need to" with "I get to" or "I want to." Then, after another minute or two, I ask them to describe how they feel about their lists now. The results are always significantly different. People say they feel:

- Excited
- Energized
- Eager

- In control
- Good
- Prepared

The tasks on the list did not change, but the words in front of them did. "I get to" or "I want to" provide a choice, empowering the person to control their day. They get to determine their attitude and actions. In other words, what we tell ourselves has a huge impact on the choices we make.

I'm reminded of this when I think of a video produced by Purple Feather called "Change Your Words. Change Your World."[3] A blind man is sitting on the street with a sign beside him displaying the following words: "I'm blind. Please help." Pedestrians stroll by, and some toss a few coins on his mat or place them in his tin cup. Others, on autopilot, walk by without acknowledging him. A young lady walks toward him, reads his sign, and keeps walking past him. Then she stops, pivots, and walks back to the man. She pulls out a marker and grabs his sign to scribble another message.

After she places the sign beside the man again, more pedestrians start giving him money. The young lady returns a while later and stands in front of the man. He recognizes it's her by the sound of her shoes. He turns his face toward her and asks, "What did you do to my sign?" She replies, "It's the same. Just different words." The sign now displays the following words: "It's a beautiful day, and I can't see it."

The words we say to ourselves significantly impact our attitudes and actions. I learned this lesson early on as an educator, and I continue to experience lessons that reinforce this fact. In disruptive, divisive, and polarizing times, we often forget about what we can control. There is so much finger-pointing and general disregard for others that it may feel like things are spiraling beyond our grasp. Educator, author, and speaker George Couros said, "We need to make the positive so loud that the negative becomes almost impossible to hear."[4]

By no means is this ignoring the negative, nor is it a message that we should have a Pollyanna approach to life. Such an approach is not only unsustainable but also inauthentic. Rather, this is a reminder that we can influence the results we get by controlling our behavior patterns and the way we think. We are in complete control of our attitudes and actions.

Tom Cody

Educational Consultant, Trainer, and Author
Top 20 Training (top20training.com)
St. Paul, Minnesota

One educator, after an honest and humbling conversation with a parent, took the initiative to change his approach toward his work, his students, and his life. It is now his mission to help others develop the skills and mindset to experience joy in their professional and personal lives. I met Tom Cody at a Jostens Renaissance National Conference a few years ago, and we have been friends ever since. Jostens Renaissance Education is a framework that helps educators create a positive school climate and culture by creating systems to enhance relationships, recognition, respect, and academic outcomes. The annual conference attracts nearly two thousand students, staff, and faculty each year. Tom is a magnet for both kids and educators! His authentic and honest approach draws you in, and his storytelling makes learning relevant.

Nobody tells you this in college as you prepare for a career in education: the single most important factor in a teacher's success or failure is their ability to manage their thinking and control their inner life during the chaos that is school.

I was a middle school and high school classroom teacher for forty years, until I retired in 2014. My career had two distinct parts. For the first twenty-five years, I spent most of my inner life in negative thinking. During the last fifteen years, I was able to maintain predominantly positive thinking. The challenges never changed. There were still special schedules, disruptive students, and jammed Xerox machines. In the latter part of my career, I simply made it a priority to take care of the inside (mindset) first and then deal with those outside conditions. Note: I never mastered this skill—there is no such thing as teacher perfection—but it was a completely different ride for both me and my students.

My story is pretty unique. I had an OMG moment back in 1998 when a parent at a conference told me their daughter hated my guts. That became a turning point for me. I started to look at some of the social-emotional learning (SEL) content that this parent was teaching in the business world. I quickly decided that I was sick and tired of being sick and tired. I was sick and tired of sleepless nights and constant apologies for my negative behavior. Then the big aha moment: I decided to shift my mindset from teaching to learning. It used to be all about me in the classroom and on the basketball court. Once I made this paradigm shift, everything changed for the better for me and the young people I was working with. I even started to teach some of these SEL skills to my students and my basketball players.

What was even more profound? My personal life changed. I became a better husband, father, son, and friend. I became more grateful, more giving. If you cannot get your mindset straightened out, you have little or no chance to succeed as an educator. A typical school day presents a constant barrage of invitations to go negative with students and fellow staff members. Metacognitive thinking means we can actually think about our thinking and do something about it when we don't like what our thinking is producing for us.

If you want to become adept at any skill, it takes practice. If you want to become better at left-handed lay-ups in basketball, you practice left-handed lay-ups. For how long? Until you master left-handed lay-ups! It's the same thing with mindset: you must practice this skill, monitor it, and shift your mindset intentionally.

My transformation led me to develop a ninth-grade SEL course at our high school. Teaching these mindset skills eventually resulted in the creation of Top 20 Training, a company that provides materials and training in this area. We have now trained over 1.5 million teachers in schools and districts all over the country.

One of our favorite Top 20 mottos is Keep Your Day! You only get this one day, today; that's all you've got for these twenty-four hours. Stop giving this day away to other negative people, to schedule changes, or to traffic jams. This mindset has drastically changed my life in positive ways. I used to be the most generous man in my school: I gave my days away to everybody! Being aware of your thinking and its impact is the greatest gift you can give to yourself.

Be GREAT Tips on Controlling Your Attitude and Actions

We make thousands of decisions a day. It's no wonder we get mentally exhausted. This fatigue can impact the choices we make concerning our attitudes and actions. German philosopher and cultural critic Friedrich Nietzsche is believed by some to have said, "When we are tired, we are attacked by the ideas we conquered long ago."[5] If you aren't getting the results you expect throughout the day, consider the following action steps:

- Establish morning and evening routines to preserve your energy for more critical and purposeful tasks throughout the day.
- Eliminate half of the items on your to-do list (if you have one) and focus on the two to three most important tasks. That way, you spend your energy on what is essential.
- Ask for help! Identify the tasks that a family member, friend, or colleague can do. You'd be surprised by who is willing to lend a helping hand.
- Do the least desirable tasks first so that you have room to operate within your strength areas throughout the day. You will be more energized and intentional.
- Show compassion for yourself and others. Seek consistency, not perfection.
- Acknowledge your emotions and identify your triggers. Emotions are real, but they are not fact.
- Identify what you control and respond accordingly.
- Gain another perspective by talking to someone you trust.

Personal skill development has become a greater priority for me during my career as an educator. To become better educators, we must strive to be effective leaders. Leadership is about influencing and motivating others regardless of title or position. In the next five chapters, you will learn how being grateful, relational, enthusiastic, authentic, and teachable will help improve your attitude and actions.

Three Questions for Conversation

1 What is the origin story of your current pattern of behavior and default thinking?

2 To gain control of your attitude and actions, what are you willing to stop doing?

3 What stories are you telling yourself that contribute to your successes or shortcomings? Are those stories accurate and still relevant?

TWO

BE GRATEFUL

*Gratitude is the single most important
ingredient to living a successful
and fulfilled life.*

—Jack Canfield

On November 13, 2020, I received the following anonymous handwritten letter in my school mailbox:

Dwight, I admire what you do for this school and our students. Quite possibly, the greatest challenge that faces us is the systemic and pervasive racism that infects our society. It stands squarely in the way of success for many of our students, and unless we can overcome it in ourselves, we can't hope to make progress toward equity for our kids. Thank you for your leadership.

I can't help but wonder why this person chose to omit their name. I also wonder what triggered them to write the letter that day. I reread it several times, trying to figure out who wrote it and if there was more to the message. Then I decided to simply be grateful for the person who put their thoughts on paper. The author of that letter recognized the challenges we are facing yet expressed their heart's desire to create conditions all students can succeed in. The letter is framed and hanging up in my office as a reminder for me to be grateful for where I am, what I am able to do, and who I work with. Being grateful can impact your perspective.

The difference between schools with a positive culture and negative culture can be observed in the behaviors of the adults, and it is felt by students and families. The results are evident. When there is a consistently high level of distress caused by strained relationships, a lack of feeling supported, and a lack of appreciation, the school culture suffers, and students are impacted. If we wait too long to recognize this, our culture can become a frustrating and ego-driven one where playing the victim is the norm. In a culture like that, very little collaboration takes place, problem solving becomes burdensome, and there's a lack of creativity and innovation. As you think about your school culture and the challenges you may be facing, consider this: What role does gratitude play in what you do and experience?

As you grapple with that question, let's focus on what it means to be grateful.

To be grateful means to consistently feel or express your appreciation of the kindness you encounter. It means to appreciate the tangible and intangible blessings each day, including family, a supportive network of friends and colleagues, and opportunities disguised as problems. Gratitude is a characteristic. Many of us were taught as children to say *please* and *thank you* as a sign of respect and to demonstrate that we were mannerly. Gratitude is easily taught, but it can quickly become an empty action if you don't understand the more profound benefits. Being grateful reflects your attitude and actions toward others. If your feelings are genuine, they will be expressed in your behavior. The author of that anonymous letter I received reflects a grateful heart, and I am certain that this person has created a positive classroom or workplace culture in their sphere of influence.

When I was a student teacher in 1994, my college professor and dear friend Dr. Robert Welker gave me some advice that I often share today. He said, "Keep a file in your desk of all the positive letters, cards, and emails you receive. When you have one of those days or weeks, reread some of them so that you remember why you became an educator." I still have that file and have created many more over the years. I have recently visited my files a few times as a reminder to appreciate the connections, experiences, and moments of gratitude shared with me. Why does this simple hack work? What is the benefit of rereading these notes and letters? It's simple: it makes us happy!

We may work with, supervise, or encounter a colleague, student, or parent who is consistently negative. They have a problem for every solution, a complaint for every compliment, and they are just a generally pessimistic person. This type of behavior can be draining. I call a person like that—who deliberately spoils the enjoyment of others through resentful or overly sober behavior—a killjoy or energy vampire. Energy vampires can destroy morale and sabotage progress. It is rare to find someone who likes being this way, so it is important to understand that they are stuck in a loop of negative thoughts that manifests through their perspective and behavior. Instead of simply telling them to be more positive, which rarely works, we must give them a strategy and show them what they can do differently.

I have found a direct link between the joy I experience and the amount of gratitude I show, think, and feel. Even though I know that gratitude can be transformational when it's practiced consistently, I often feel frustrated. I think about what stands in the way of me being more grateful. The answer is quite simple: I care deeply about education and the growth, development, and overall well-being of students and educators. I see barriers that I alone can't remove or that are embedded in our system so that the task seems impossible.

Over the years, I noticed that my frustration masked many emotions. A good friend of mine named Steve Bollar shared something with me several years ago that is applicable to many educators. He said, "Vision frustrates your present but excites your future."

Frustration can be a barrier to gratitude. We may live in a constant state of frustration because we have a vivid image of what our schools can become as we remove barriers to allow teachers to teach, students to learn, and families to become partners in developing the whole child. We can imagine developing relevant learning activities that will fully engage students. Innovation is abundant. It's not just shiny toys; it's ingenious thinking that solves long-standing problems. We can imagine timely, tangible, and meaningful recognition of student and staff success. We can imagine teachers who empower student choice and who give students a voice in the learning process. However, we also face the reality of unfunded mandates that take us in the opposite direction of our vision. We face an overemphasis on standardized testing to measure what students know and can do. We are confronted with the reality of exhausted staff members who cannot take one more thing being added to their plate.

As we share our excitement about our schools' futures, we may frustrate our colleagues. They may feel depleted, stressed, and overwhelmed, and they may simply want to get through the day. We may share ideas, instructional strategies, and articles that challenge their thinking and slowly push them out of their comfort zones. We may ask profound questions that require more than a simple yes or no response. We may question current practices so we can learn more about the *why*—challenging the status quo while trying to manage the emotions that come from being pushed, gently or not so gently, to do things differently. Yes, we can frustrate others, just as our present situation frustrates us. We must keep this in mind as we navigate through these challenging yet exciting times in education.

When I embrace my frustration, I take a moment to express my gratitude for the willingness to adjust. I express my appreciation for friends and colleagues I can reach out to. I am grateful to them for helping me to stop my negative thought cycle, and I appreciate when they share an encouraging word that allows me to become more solution focused. I remember to be grateful for the progress we make toward our goals, the connections we make with students and staff, and the positive stories that occur every day in our schools. One of the simplest and easiest ways to overcome frustration is to be grateful.

The level of gratitude we show influences the culture we create in our schools, classrooms, and homes. School culture consists of the values, traditions, rituals, and routines established by adults. In other words, how educators behave defines school culture, and then students adapt to that culture. Schools become stressful due to the speed of change, increasing expectations, and shifting standards. But it doesn't have to be that way if we take responsibility for the type of culture we want to create. We can begin that process by owning the problem. According to best-selling author and educator Gay Hendricks, "Stress and conflict are caused by resisting acceptance and ownership. If there is any part of ourselves or our lives that we're not fully willing to accept, we will experience stress and friction in that area. The stress will disappear the moment we accept that part and claim ownership of it."[1] By owning the problem, we can be grateful for the lessons we learn and the skills we develop as we put in the work to make changes. However, negativity may still creep in like a thief.

Thankfully, I can count on one hand the number of times someone stole something from me. Regardless of how often it's happened, I felt violated, frustrated, and angry. The audacity required for someone to take something that doesn't belong to them is baffling. And another type of thievery exists, perpetrated by those who intentionally or unintentionally steal joy, happiness, or peace from others. They don't just steal it; they rob it. The difference between a thief and a robber is proximity. Thieves take things when no one is around. They sneak up and look for opportunities to pounce so they can leave unseen and unheard. Robbers have little regard for the individual and, yielding to their arrogance or greed, forcibly take what they believe they should have. Both are selfish acts.

These thieves disguise themselves as policymakers, concerned friends and parents, naysayers, or so-called realists. They can also appear daily in the form of social media posts, phone calls, and headlines. They lurk among us with a critical eye, waiting to suck the life out of a well-thought-out lesson plan, creatively designed unit, or new idea, all in the name of preserving the past or fear of change. They unknowingly limit risk taking. They steal joy with words of doubt, critiquing in the form of unsolicited feedback or a relentless list of rhetorical questions. After a while, it requires too much energy to fend them off—energy that should be used on something productive or positive. It has taken me time to own my attitude and actions toward others when I am in the presence of thieves or am the thief myself. Talk about a hard revelation! But there are four things we can do to respond positively:

- **Make sure you are not a thief.** Check your attitude and actions. When others enthusiastically share ideas or take calculated risks to try something new, listen attentively, be encouraging, and identify ways you can support them. If you experience negative emotions, remember that your feelings are real, but they aren't fact. Examine where your feelings come from and why you're experiencing them, and be grateful for your growth.
- **Recharge your battery daily.** You have a finite amount of will-power each day. When your resolve is low, you tend to have a less than positive attitude and behave differently. Recognize the stress points and take ownership of your behavior. Focus on things that energize you. Get the necessary rest so you can face new challenges the next day. Express gratitude for the

day's positive experiences and lessons learned from the negative experiences.

- **Develop a personal learning network.** Connect with trusted colleagues who believe in you. These critical friends will help you become the best you can be. Identify an accountability partner to remind you to practice gratitude and change your behavior.
- **Become a trusted and critical friend to a colleague in your building.** Booker T. Washington said, "If you want to lift yourself up, lift someone else."[2] Your experience can be a valuable resource for others and the support they need to grow.

Another barrier to gratitude is our ego. Ego is the antithesis of gratitude. When you are driven by ego, you behave in ways that prevent gratitude. Ego is focused on self-preservation, which manifests as being unwilling to take responsibility for your actions, blaming others for your mistakes and how you feel, and taking almost everything personally. When you consistently behave in these ways, you are not open to others, which can harm the positive school culture you envision. Here are some examples of what this may look like:

- You blame the previous teacher or grade level for the lack of student success instead of focusing on what you can do to help students progress and achieve.
- You believe the building or district administration doesn't care about you because you disagree with the schedule chosen during a crisis (such as the COVID-19 pandemic).
- You hoard ideas, lesson plans, and successful activities instead of sharing them with grade level or department colleagues.
- You refuse to ask for help when you don't know how to use a new application, software, or learning management system, so you blame your failure on whoever "forced" you to make the change.

- You don't communicate with parents because you aren't confident in your instructional strategies or decision-making, or you believe they are against you.
- You don't engage in discussions during staff meetings because you fear what your colleagues may think of you.
- You focus your attention and blame on barriers to student success that you can't control, such as family dynamics, socioeconomic status, etc.
- You get defensive when asked about a decision you made, an outcome you got, or a question you asked.
- You believe you can do things better than others; therefore, you judge their actions instead of learning from their experience.

I worked with a teacher who let her ego get in the way of her performance. She was once a good teacher who had great rapport with students. She was respected by her colleagues, had a depth of content knowledge, and captivated her students with a combination of storytelling, experience, and questioning techniques. Over time, I noticed a shift in her behavior. I started getting complaints from her colleagues, her students, and their parents that she was ill prepared, disinterested in class, and visibly disengaged during meetings.

I met with her several times to check on her well-being and share some of the concerns brought to my attention. Each time, her response was the same: "I'm fine; everything is good." Each time, I reminded her that it was OK if she wasn't fine and that we could help. I made a few suggestions, we worked together on an action plan to help her improve, and she said she was going to enlist the help of a couple of her colleagues who were eager to support her. Over time, she refused their help and continued to make excuses about her performance, all the while saying that she was OK. She failed to meet the conditions of her action plan and chose to resign. That was a sad day because I was watching someone's ego—defensiveness, a failure to take responsibility, and refusal to accept help from others who loved her—get in the way of her becoming an outstanding educator. She had some problems yet made excuses that prevented her from making progress.

One of my roommates during my freshman year of college used to recite a line from a Greek fraternity poem so much that I learned it myself: "Excuses are tools of incompetence, and those who use them seldom amount to anything else." Making excuses is our brain's way of protecting us from perceived or real danger. When faced with a barrier or obstacle, be it physical, emotional, or mental, our brain's natural response is to tell us to fight the threat, flee from the danger, or freeze in front of it. Practicing gratitude is a way to hijack our emotional reactions so that we can respond more positively. To Be GREAT, eliminate the excuses, accept responsibility for your attitude and actions, and create the conditions for you and others to succeed.

The third barrier to gratitude is playing the victim. A few years ago, I found myself blaming others for the lack of joy I was experiencing as a building principal—and in my life in general. My ego was in overdrive, my joy was artificial or nonexistent, and I blamed others often. I was in a rut of negative self-talk that was emotionally and mentally exhausting. At the time, there was a lot of buzz about Todd Whitaker's book *Shifting the Monkey: The Art of Protecting Good People from Liars, Criers, and Other Slackers,*[3] so I decided to read it. He is one of my favorite authors on all things concerning education and education leadership.

For those who are not familiar with the phrase "shifting the monkey," it's about the many burdens, or monkeys, we may carry on our backs. Sometimes we place these monkeys on our own backs; sometimes others dump their monkeys on our backs. We may even allow them to do so, especially if we're in leadership roles. This can be a form of enabling. Whether this happens intentionally or unintentionally is not that important. What is important is that we can answer the following three questions to help improve our schools, classrooms, homes, and organizations:

- Where is the monkey? (Identification)
- Where should it be? (Ownership)
- How do I get it there? (Accountability)

Instead of continuing to make excuses, I recognized that my ego was the cause of my excuse making. My lack of gratitude led to a cycle of negative storytelling in my head that may have harmed our school culture because, as leadership expert John C. Maxwell wrote, "Everything rises and falls on leadership."[4] I learned the following lessons:

- We notoriously lean on the best people to get things done. This can lead to fatigue, frustration, and burnout. We must hold everyone in the organization accountable for what they are supposed to do.
- When confronting negative behaviors, we must maintain a level of respect for everyone by not taking things personally. Taking things personally is a sign of ego-driven action. The goal should be to teach what is expected to help the individual be better. We all want to be respected, appreciated, and encouraged.
- When faced with negative behaviors, confront them. When we are afraid to do so, we allow "bad people" to shift their monkeys onto the backs of the people bothered by their behavior, destroying morale, creating an adverse climate, and lessening risk taking during collaborative learning experiences. Don't act afraid. Respectfully confront the behavior by asking the person to talk immediately after the class, meeting, etc., and move on. I've done this, and it works. I was also the recipient of such a request when I lashed out at one of my colleagues during a district administrative team meeting. I was quickly called to the carpet, and I certainly had a monkey on my back for the rest of the meeting! However, I respected my leader for addressing my behavior privately and respectfully. I apologized to him and my colleague, and we moved on.

- Communicating expectations eliminates confusion, makes expectations easier to fulfill, and reduces excuse making.

- What is recognized and rewarded is repeated. This goes for both negative and positive behaviors. Ego-driven behaviors such as pouting, complaining, gossiping, and bulldozing often continue because we cater to these behaviors. Ignore them. Think about that person in your life who pouts whenever they don't get what they want. If you give in to this reaction, you only reinforce that pouting gets them what they want. To ignore it simply means that you see it happen, but you don't back down from what you expect of this person. It's easier said than done, but again, this can significantly improve school climate and culture.

- Sometimes no response is a response that sends a clear message. For example, if someone tries to interject a joke while someone else is speaking, merely ignoring that person will show them and others that the behavior is not acceptable at that time. This keeps the monkey on the back of the jokester, not on you or others in the room. A person who jokes at inappropriate times may be internally making excuses for future behavior. Make a note of that.

- When you confront and blame an entire group of people because it feels safer than addressing the few people doing something negative, two things happen. First, you put monkeys on the backs of great educators or students who feel guilty because they think you are talking about them. Second, the guilty people believe you are talking about someone else. In the end, the behavior doesn't change.

When we practice gratitude, our victim mentality will diminish because we will be more focused on taking responsibility for our emotional state, thoughts, and actions. Our victim mentality will be transformed into one that is open to serving others. According to author Deepak

Chopra, "You are genuinely grateful when your ego gets out of the way. Real gratitude isn't passing and temporary. Gratitude takes openness and the willingness to set your ego aside. No one is grateful for things they think they deserve. Therefore, gratitude is unearned, like grace. When it is deeply felt, gratitude applies to everything, not simply to goodies that come your way."[5]

The entertainment company SoulPancake made a heartwarming video that explains the science of gratitude.[6] It begins with a guy named Julian Huguet dressed in a lab coat looking into the camera as he describes the reason for the experiment, saying, "Psychologists have scientifically proven that one of the greatest contributing factors to overall happiness in your life is how much gratitude you show." They select a few random people and ask them several questions to measure their levels of happiness. Afterward, each participant is asked about the person who had the most significant impact on their life—someone who has done something extraordinary for them. They are asked to close their eyes and think about that person. Next, they are given a pen and paper and asked to write that person a letter explaining why they are important.

Some of the volunteers include a mother, an older sister, a sibling, and a best friend. Julian throws them a curveball when he tells them they will call their person and read the letter to them. Each person picks up the receiver, waits for an answer, and begins reading the letter. Some laugh, some cry, but each has a smile on their face.

There is an older gentleman, possibly in his midseventies, who is soft-spoken, calm, and nurturing. Julian asks him who he chose, and he says, "My college accounting instructor." Julian is shocked and interested in learning more. He asks if they're still in contact, but the gentleman confirms his professor is no longer alive. Julian asks him to read his letter aloud, and he does: "The person who has had the greatest influence in my life, besides Jesus Christ, is my college accounting instructor. He had a joy and excitement about his job more than any teacher I have ever known." Next to this gentlemen's personal Savior, his *teacher* was the most influential person in his life!

An educator's influence is immortal. We cannot forget that. To remind ourselves of the immortality of our influence, we must establish a practice of gratitude.

Practice of Gratitude

In chapter 1, I explained that we only control two things in our lives: our attitude and our actions. There are two critical points in the SoulPancake video mentioned above. First, to increase your happiness level, you must establish a *practice* of gratitude, not just have an attitude of gratitude. Both are beneficial, but one leads to increased happiness. Vulnerability researcher Dr. Brené Brown wrote, "The relationship between joy and gratitude was one of the important things I found in my research. . . . I did not interview one person who had described themselves as joyful who also did not actively practice gratitude. For me, it was very counterintuitive because I went into the research thinking that the relationship between joy and gratitude was: if you are joyful, you should be grateful. But it wasn't that way at all."[7]

As the SoulPancake video ends, Julian points out that all the participants' happiness levels increased by about 2 percent after thinking and writing about the person they were most grateful to. However, their happiness levels grew exponentially when they called the person to tell them. This action led to an increase of 4 percent to 19 percent happiness!

Gratitude is merely taking time to think about all the positive things in your life. And that's a start. But to Be GREAT, I encourage you to develop a practice of gratitude. To practice gratitude, make it a part of an actionable daily ritual or routine. Practice develops muscle memory that will essentially lead to new behavior. It requires moving beyond merely thinking about gratitude, which is still beneficial, to behaving in a certain way. Many of our thoughts run on autopilot or follow an established pattern of thinking. Research suggests that a whopping 80 percent of our thoughts are negative, and 95 percent of these thoughts are on a continuous loop.[8]

For example, educators have a pattern of thinking and behaving when it comes to the average school calendar. As we gear up for a new school year, August is filled with excitement about starting over, anxiety about the preparation, fear of the unknown, and anticipation of the first few school days. After we settle into the first three to four weeks of the school year, we start thinking about the end of the quarter and what it takes to wrap things up, our minds cluttered with thoughts about grades, contacting families, designing or grading assessments, and the amount of time it takes to complete these tasks. We transition to the second quarter and soon count down the days to winter break and exams (depending on grade level).

We return from break and dread the long, dark days of winter. Our minds are overcome with the cycle of "hurry up and wait" for the next vacation. We think that students will behave more negatively, and we believe we'll face more distractions. When spring break comes, we eagerly anticipate better weather, more daylight, and a few months left in the school year. When the year ends, we repeat the cycle.

Being grateful can rewire our brains to create a new loop that is more positive. To improve our attitude and actions, we must focus on the benefits of practicing gratitude. Without understanding the benefits, we have no foundation to stand on and succumb to the ebb and flow of life. We want to establish a culture that is more positive, pleasant, kind, and optimistic. This reminds me of legendary educator Dr. Rita Pierson, who said, "Kids don't learn from people they don't like."[9] Even though Dr. Pierson was talking about a specific colleague and her technique with her students, the idea is that it's easier to learn from those who are pleasant, who are easy to approach, and who seem to enjoy what they do.

One tangible way to establish a practice of gratitude is to give handwritten notes or gifts to others. Early in my career as an administrator,

I learned the Jostens Renaissance results formula. As I shared in the previous chapter, Jostens Renaissance Education is a framework that helps educators create a positive school climate and culture by creating systems to enhance relationships, recognition, respect, and academic outcomes. The framework focuses on defining expectations and recognizing and rewarding students, staff, and faculty for their positive behavior. This is accomplished through a practice of gratitude, praise, and celebration, and it creates a positive school culture. The formula consists of the five R's:[10]

- **Respect:** Identify and communicate what behaviors you respect and value in your school or classroom.
- **Recognize:** Acknowledge and highlight those who demonstrate the behaviors and values you respect.
- **Reward:** Verbally praise or give a small token of recognition to those who demonstrate what is valued and respected.
- **Reinforce:** Recognizing and rewarding reinforces what is respected and valued.
- **Results:** What is respected, recognized, rewarded, and reinforced increases your positive outcomes and leads to better results.

I wanted to show my gratitude for my staff, so I purchased a bag of gold star lapel pins, found some inexpensive cards with our school's logo on them, and periodically wrote thank-you notes to educators who modeled our core values. After I would write a note and seal the envelope, I would attach one of the gold star lapel pins to it. Then, as I walked around the building, I would hand the cards to the recipients or place them in their mailboxes. I would often see the stars pinned on their lanyards, name badges, or shirts. I would also see the notes prominently displayed on their desks or in their classrooms. It was important to me to be specific about what I was grateful for. Those notes and pins were a huge hit, and they cost little to no money and very little time. I remember one teacher bragging that he was a five-star general because he had five stars pinned on his name badge! That teacher consistently went above and beyond to do what was best for kids, and he felt valued, seen, and appreciated. However, I probably gained more from the experience than the recipients because it felt good to do something nice for someone and express why I was grateful for them.

The older gentleman in the SoulPancake video may have spoken about what he learned from his professor, but what was highlighted was how his professor did his job: with joy and excitement every day. His behavior was contagious and made a lasting impression on this student. It may be challenging to show happiness and excitement these days. But we can control our attitude by practicing gratitude. Character is revealed, not developed, during challenging times. We've met some challenging events in the past few years, but we will continue to model the skills necessary for success as we practice more gratitude.

These are formative years in the lives of students. Educators often fall into the trap of counting the days until the end of the school year. While this may encourage some, it may also send a subtle message that school is a place to escape from rather than a place to experience. Let's remember not to count down the days; let's instead tally the opportunities we have to positively change lives and impact futures.

Kim Strobel

Educator, Speaker, and Happiness Coach
Strobel Education (strobeleducation.com)
Tell City, Indiana

An important benefit of being grateful is increased levels of happiness. One educator who used gratitude to pivot in her career is Kim Strobel, happiness coach. I learned about Kim while listening to her interview on Steve Bollar's podcast, the *Stand Tall Leadership Show*.[11] I was intrigued by her title and drawn in by her story.

I am quick to let others know that becoming a happiness coach came from my own darkness, my own trauma, my own years of intense and silent suffering. And because of this, I'm pretty sure becoming a happiness coach was birthed in my heart and soul even if I had to go through hell to birth her. I suffered from a debilitating illness known as panic disorder with agoraphobia. I was scared to leave my house or even drive my car five minutes to work. The roots of it were in my childhood, but I developed the full-blown version of it at age sixteen. I suffered greatly from it until around the age of twenty-four, when I finally got a proper diagnosis and did a mixture of therapy and Zoloft. Because of this, I dove into the self-help field and have been studying happiness and personal development ever since. I'm on a mission to help others know they can do hard things and still find joy and happiness.

I admire Kim for recognizing that she needed help and taking the initiative to learn all she could about ways to cultivate gratitude. She not only made it a lifestyle but also turned it into a career so she could help others. She reminds us that there is a direct correlation between gratitude and positive psychology.

Gratitude is one of the top five research-based happiness habits that can increase our baseline happiness. The average human being has about seventy thousand thoughts a day. Of those seventy thousand thoughts, 80 percent are negative. Since most of us are average human beings, this means we are having fifty-six thousand negative thoughts every single day. Think back to this morning when you got out of bed. Some of you had fifty-five negative thoughts before you even made it to the bathroom. As soon as the alarm went off, you thought, "I didn't get enough sleep." Or maybe you thought, "I don't want to go to work today."

And then you got up, and you started walking to the bathroom and told yourself that your knees hurt. Then you looked in the mirror and said, "Shoot, I have a fever blister." Then you put your pants on, silently grimaced, and said, "I'm getting so fat." The bottom line is we have these thoughts, and for many of us they're running on default all the time, so we don't even notice them. Over a decade of empirical studies has proved that gratitude has a profound effect on the way our brains are wired.

Like the person who wrote me the anonymous letter I mentioned at the beginning of this chapter, we can take the time to express gratitude. We can write down at least three things we are thankful for each day. This can greatly impact our level of happiness, improve our connections with others, and make our jobs more enjoyable. In fact, we can rewire our brains.

When you consistently write down three things you are thankful for each day, you begin to create a new neural feedback loop in your brain. I want you to imagine that you have all these roads in your brain—hundreds and hundreds of roads. And whatever road you travel the most is the road with the deepest grooves, which means it's the one you come back to most easily. For example, some of us have a road in our brain that constantly tells us how much we hate our body, how unhappy we are in our marriage, or how frustrated we are with our job. And the more we travel down that road, the deeper that groove becomes, until we default to going down that darn road every time. If you can incorporate a two-minute daily gratitude practice, you can create a new neural feedback loop in your brain. You can actually change from a pessimist into an optimist after about thirty days.

Consider keeping a gratitude journal and implementing this practice at your school. Some like to purchase an actual journal, such as the *Five Minute Journal*.[12] When I was battling my second bout of chronic depression, a colleague and friend bought me a copy. While I truly appreciated it, honestly, keeping a journal was the last thing I wanted to do. I didn't have the energy and didn't want to exercise the daily discipline a journal required. So it sat in my work bag for about a month. One day I was feeling especially low, and when I opened my bag to grab my laptop, there was the journal. I opened it and actually took time to read the first few pages. There are no writing prompts or arduous steps, and it literally takes five minutes to complete. This journal provides spaces to list three things you're grateful for, state your intentions for each day, write down affirmations, and highlight positive experiences at the end of each day. At first, I thought it was a little woo-woo or new age, but it does work and is backed by research. A word of caution: to avoid making this one more task to complete, focus on the act of writing for your own good, not a part of a daily "to-do" list. That way, if you don't do it, you don't shame or judge yourself for "failing to complete a task." If you miss a day, move on. It doesn't mean you weren't grateful that day. It just means you didn't write it down. Nothing more, nothing less.

Megan Anderson

Assistant Principal
Cherry Hill Primary
Washington Court House, Ohio

Megan Anderson is a highly energetic and intelligent servant leader who exudes gratitude. She doesn't see an obstacle she can't overcome, and she genuinely cares about others. However, there was one obstacle she had to overcome that she did not anticipate.

"When your feet hit the ground in the morning, do you tell yourself, 'I am worthy'?"

This question was posed on a brisk January morning while I was attending an education summit on the campus of The Ohio State University. It was a reality check for me. As I sat in the room with my back against the chair and my feet touching the ground, my thoughts were silent. The question had left me utterly speechless. To be honest, telling others how much I loved and admired them was always a priority. This servant leadership mentality was ingrained in me from the time I was born. I placed others first.

"What words are you personally feeding yourself?" The timing of this presenter's message was impeccable; I could have sworn he was zoned in on me, but I know many of the other educators in that room felt as I did. It was during this moment of the presentation that time stood still.

I began reminiscing about my early years as a student. I had struggled academically, my physique growing up was "too muscular," and I was often called "manly" by other girls. I scored a 15 on the ACT in high school, which was considered too low; therefore, I wasn't accepted into my first-choice college. Fast-forward several years and I found myself consumed by the world of research, trying to find out more information about the rare genetic mutation my daughter was born with. The torrent of words I had used to tear myself apart over the years finally came to a halt, and it was at that moment I wondered how many other women felt this way.

What kind of culture was I building in my house, my work? I wasn't grateful for myself and who I was created to be. Some may have overlooked me, but I needed to embrace that I was chosen for this journey. To be honest, I was so consumed with the go-go-go business of survival that I had lost myself. I had lost the moments in which I should have been grateful. I needed to teach myself how to rewire my brain so that I could help create a culture of gratitude in other people's lives that would empower them. I knew it needed to start with me. It needed to start with the positive words of affirmation that I would tell myself every morning when my feet touched the ground.

Megan eliminated excuses and worked on herself so that she could become an even more genuine servant leader. She examined the messages she told herself, realized that she didn't believe she was enough, and became intentional about practicing gratitude. When she became an assistant principal, she took steps to make gratitude a part of her school's culture. The following is a gratitude practice she implemented at her school.

Cultivating Gratitude in Your Building

Begin every week by emailing all staff a Monday Morning Mindfulness and Motivational form that includes this list of activities. Staff can choose to do any of the following:

- Share a positive quote.
- Provide a multiple-choice mental health check-in.
- Celebrate success stories from classrooms.
- Share a brief mindfulness breathing video.

Thank your staff for opening up to you, Megan suggests. They will feel your authenticity when you reach out to them and be grateful that you checked in on them. Create notes of gratitude containing puns for all staff with a small gift that ties into each week's creative pun. Change which day of the week you send the gratitude notes to ensure it's something your staff will look forward to. This will keep things from becoming stale. Expand on the principle of these gratitude gifts by having your staff write notes to themselves or give heart stickers to teachers on Valentine's Day.

Megan's gratitude practice shows how creating a culture of gratitude simply takes consistent and intentional effort. Anyone in the building can take the lead. It is important, however, for the leader to actively participate because others will determine if they should participate based on what they observe the leader doing.

According to researcher, detective, and NYPD Mental Health and Wellness Coordinator Dr. Jeff Thompson, "Gratitude practices help you manage these tough times, and it reminds you that if you stop and pause, there is still good all around us, and it is happening each day. Think of the alternative. What if we ignore the good in our lives and only concentrate on the bad things that occur each day? This is not healthy, and that fear, anxiety, depression, and stress will destroy us mentally and physically."[13]

Dr. Thompson describes the negative consequences of ignoring the good in our lives, but what are some tangible benefits of practicing gratitude? And what is the impact on school culture? Here are some benefits of practicing gratitude:[14]

- It improves your physical health. People who exhibit gratitude physically feel better, they exercise more, and they go to the doctor for more frequent checkups.
- It improves your psychological health. Grateful people enjoy higher levels of well-being and happiness and suffer fewer symptoms of depression.
- It stands out. When you feel gratitude, it often overpowers other feelings.
- It's contagious. When you feel gratitude for one thing in your life, it tends to overflow into other parts of your life—even parts that you thought weren't deserving of gratitude.

- It enhances empathy and reduces aggression. Those who show their gratitude are less likely to seek revenge against others and more likely to behave in a sensitive, prosocial manner.
- It improves your sleep. Practicing gratitude regularly can help you sleep longer and better.
- It enhances your self-esteem. People who are grateful have increased self-esteem, partly due to their ability to appreciate other people's accomplishments.
- It increases mental strength. Grateful people have enhanced resilience and an advantage in overcoming trauma, helping them to bounce back from highly stressful situations.

School culture is defined as the beliefs, traditions, and norms that adults create and consistently model. Before instituting another program to improve your school or classroom culture, consider what part gratitude plays in your established practices.

Be GREAT Tips on How to Be Grateful

To grow in gratitude, I encourage you to cultivate a practice of it. To cultivate means to prepare the ground for crops or gardening, which is indicative of multiple steps and an ongoing process. To be more grateful, I advise you to try the following:

- Besides simply praying before a meal, pray or meditate throughout the day.
- Spend five minutes a day writing down three things you're grateful for.
- Spend a few minutes in class one day a week asking students to share what they're most grateful for.
- Spend more time with friends.
- Accentuate the positive more often by celebrating your success and the successes of others.
- Minimize the to-do list.

- Create a to-be list.
- Take responsibility for your actions instead of playing the victim.

Three Questions for Conversation

1 What is your gratitude baseline? The Gratitude Quiz from *Greater Good Magazine* can help you define it.[15] Once you get the results, identify just one thing you can do differently to express more gratitude—and then do it intentionally on a consistent basis.

2 How will a practice of gratitude change your response to feedback or constructive criticism? To answer this question, start by considering how you typically respond—and why.

3 In what ways will you apply a gratitude practice in your school or classroom?

THREE

BE RELATIONAL

*To inspire meaningful change, you must
make a connection to the heart before
you can make a connection to the mind.*

—George Couros

We lead people—not programs, platforms, and positions. If we don't connect with people, nothing else really matters, or it doesn't matter for long. Having positive relationships is a foundational principle for educators and leaders like you. When I walked into my first education class my freshman year at Wittenberg University, I saw the following words written in the middle of the expansive black chalkboard:

No significant learning occurs without a significant relationship.
—Dr. James Comer

Those words provided so much clarity. Instantly, I was certain about my career choice. I thought about the teachers and coaches I had growing up. I thought about certain neighbors and parents of my childhood friends, who cared for us like we were their own kids. I thought about the village my mom created to help her guide us in the right direction. We didn't always appreciate it, like it, or understand it, but looking back on it now, I would not have it any other way. It all made sense, and those words clearly and concisely described why I wanted to become an educator. Through positive relationships with my students, I could positively their change lives and impact their futures.

Not all students have a village. Not all students feel that they have one educator who truly believes in them and with whom they have a trusting relationship. You may not have had that experience yourself. Yet you want your students to have it.

Relational describes how two or more people are *connected*. Relational is an action word indicating an ongoing process that requires intentionality. Nothing just happens, especially when it comes to establishing positive relationships. To be relational is an act of service, and for some, it's a way of life. Meaningful relationships are transformational, not transactional. In a transactional relationship, one party is seeking to gain from another at a cost. One of the people involved is acting out of self-interest, and little value is placed on the relationship.

It's no secret that creating and maintaining positive relationships contributes to overall success and growth. The foundation of our work goes far beyond having content knowledge, pedagogy, and understanding of assessment. Those things are no doubt important to becoming an effective educator. Still, without having positive relationships, you can be the best technical educator and have no significant impact on your students and colleagues. You show me a school with toxic or negative relationships, and I guarantee it is not a successful school. While we focus on relationships with others, we cannot neglect the relationship we have with ourselves.

Your Most Important Human Relationship

The most important human relationship we have is the relationship with ourselves. How we treat ourselves can lead to success or sabotage. There is a growing body of research about the importance of self-care, primarily because our culture has glorified busyness and glamorized the grind. We wear busyness as a badge of honor and work ourselves to the point of exhaustion. We engage in conversations about how busy we are, and we story top to ensure we are the busiest in our group. We equate busyness with productivity and develop a martyr mindset. It's self-destructive and models to our students, family members, and communities that what we do is arduous, burdensome work. We are taught that rugged individualism is the pathway to success. Happiness researcher, author, and speaker Shawn Achor wrote, "First as children, then as adults in the workplace, we are conditioned to disproportionately value things we accomplish on our own."[1] During my first year as a principal of my own building, I went in excited about changing things up. I didn't do a great job of listening to the veteran staff and began implementing initiatives without any input and collaboration. I had one of the best assistant principals in the area, yet I felt that as the principal, I had to lead on my own. I quickly learned that my ego was going to leave me standing alone rather than standing among my staff. I had to ask myself, "Is that the message I want to send? Do I want to work myself to exhaustion and eventually burn out?"

We often say that students are the most important people in the building. We also say that we must always do what is best for them, especially when making decisions about curriculum, instruction, assessment, and culture. Our students are why we do what we do, but they are not the most important people in the building. We are.

Our attitude and mental well-being affect the climate and culture of our schools. That's a great deal of pressure, and we can sabotage ourselves with self-destructive thoughts. Sometimes our greatest enemy or barrier to success is ourselves. Past experiences, negative self-talk, or even replaying others' negative words can sabotage our ideas, goals, and dreams.

Several years ago, I had the chance to hear Liz Murray, author of *Breaking Night: A Memoir of Forgiveness, Survival, and My Journey from Homeless to Harvard*, share her story. Her life story was made into a Lifetime movie titled *Homeless to Harvard: The Liz Murray Story*. As I listened, I frantically wrote down and tweeted nuggets of wisdom that she shared. One message emerged loud and clear: she chose not to self-destruct. There have been several times in my life when I have thought or spoken destructive thoughts or words to myself that sabotaged my dreams, diminished my hope, and hurt how I connected with others. There are ten ideas that continue to help me overcome self-destruction and foster a positive relationship with myself. You may find them helpful as well:

- When you feel like giving up, acknowledge these feelings, embrace them, and then do the opposite. This is easier said than done, but each of us has reached major and minor milestones by simply not giving up.
- Rely on past actions that led to successes in your life and celebrate what you've accomplished. Think about the process and simply apply the lessons learned.
- We are imperfect people with many faults. Acknowledge your faults, but don't dwell on them.

- When we walk into a room, the energy either goes up or goes down. Those in the room either feel encouraged or discouraged; no one stays the same. Either way, our presence makes a difference. With that in mind, when you look in the mirror or think about who you are, focus on the things you do that positively change lives and impact others. Self-destruction is also destructive to those you interact with.

- We are not guaranteed time, so whatever your dreams are, write them down, establish a plan, and *do something*. Better yet, just do something and develop the plan as you go. Excuses are self-destructive and waste time. If you wait for perfect conditions to get started, you'll never get anything done. Replace the *yeah, buts* with *yes, and*.

- Choose action over talk, curiosity over complaints, and solutions over massaging the problems. You'll be amazed by how much better you feel and how much you accomplish. Additionally, your circle of influence will be even greater!

- Self-destructive behaviors prevent us from being keenly aware of those around us because we selfishly focus on our faults. We must open our eyes, ears, and minds to people around us. Embrace experiences and be receptive to new ideas, new adventures, exciting books, or opportunities to serve others. We must invest in ourselves so that we can be the people who influence others' lives for the better.

- Become a great student of yourself. Learn and do something new each day, week, month, and year. Live your life! If you have no preconceived notions of what is supposed to happen, you have no barriers holding you back and no doubt. Learn along the way and enjoy the process!

- Ask and answer the *what if* question. You don't know what will happen if you only think about it. There are no statues of people who simply thought great things—there are statues of people who did them.

- Finding your passion provides purpose in your life. Just think about those times when you were exhausted but suddenly got a burst of energy because you had to do what you are most passionate about. It doesn't mean the work will be easy, but it will be meaningful.

You are in a position to impact teachers' and students' lives every day. That type of power has a lot to do with your relationship with yourself and how that influences your attitude and actions. How you consistently show up creates culture because your behavior informs the norms, values, and traditions that others rely on.

Relationships with Others

As we learn to have a more positive relationship with ourselves, we can apply the same principles to help others. This is not without challenges, though. Our world is more complicated than ever due to the rapid pace of change, growing polarization, diminishing civility, and pressure to do more. The schoolhouse remains a place where we can help students develop the skills to establish positive relationships with others and significantly impact our world. We need community, and we need each other. Shawn Achor wrote, "But while we all need periods of solitude from time to time in order to reflect and recharge, isolation is never the cure for what ails us in life. As human beings, we are wired to be tribal creatures rather than lone wolves; ever since the days of the hunter-gatherers we have desperately needed one another in order to survive."

Having positive relationships creates a biological response. For example, your brain produces oxytocin, also known as the love hormone. It feels good to be loved! You feel emotionally safe, and you feel that you belong. When this happens, your brain is open to new ideas, you combat the stress hormone cortisol, you embrace cognitive challenges, and you feel connected to others. The more you feel valued, the more you feel respected. The more you feel respected, the more you contribute. Positive relationships prepare the brain to learn and lead, and the result is more positive outcomes. The process of establishing positive relationships is dynamic and nuanced. However, there are several characteristics or behaviors that help you create positive relationships.

Trust

My third-grade teacher, Ms. Penny Sanecki, embodied the words of Dr. James Comer. I loved Ms. Sanecki! I wasn't a confident student my first few years of school. I was shy and timid, but I felt like Ms. Sanecki saw me. One day, while I was completing my multiplication tables, she saw me using my fingers instead of trying to figure out the answers in my head. She walked to my desk, knelt beside me, and jokingly said, "You know how to do these. You can do it." She smiled at me and walked away. From that day on, I worked extremely hard for her. She would consistently affirm my effort and progress. Her belief went beyond my math skills. She gave me more challenging books to read. She saw me as a leader, not as the shy, timid kid that I saw. She made me feel like I belonged in her class, and her consistent positive behavior created the conditions for me to trust her. She had my best interest in mind. Because I felt connected, valued, and respected, I was ready to learn every day.

Ms. Sanecki changed the trajectory of my life, and for that, I am forever grateful. I trusted her. Several researchers assert that trust is the foundation of successful work cultures. The same goes for personal relationships. According to child psychiatrist Dr. Pamela Cantor, "Positive developmental relationships are characterized by attunement, warmth, consistency, co-regulation, and an adult's ability to perceive accurately and respond to a child's internal state. In other words, positive relationships are not just about being nice to a student. They're about building trust."[2] Trust is one of the essential principles required to establish positive relationships and a positive culture. Without it, the best you can expect is compliance. With it, you are guaranteed commitment.

You cannot take establishing and maintaining trust for granted. The more volatile, uncertain, complex, and ambiguous our world becomes, the more likely you will become disenchanted, discouraged, and disengaged. Trust is foundational for the success of any working relationship. And it takes intentional work.

In an article called "The Neuroscience of Trust," author Paul J. Zak stated, "In my research I've found that building a culture of trust is what makes a meaningful difference. Employees in high-trust organizations are more productive, have more energy at work, collaborate better with their colleagues, and stay with their employers longer than people working at low-trust companies. They also suffer less chronic stress and are happier with their lives, and these factors fuel stronger performance. . . . Compared with people at low-trust companies, people at high-trust companies report: 74% less stress, 106% more energy at work, 50% higher productivity, 13% fewer sick days, 76% more engagement, 29% more satisfaction with their lives, 40% less burnout."[3] But what exactly is trust, and how do we go about establishing trusting relationships? Three components make up trust: character, connection, and competence.[4]

The character component of trust simply means consistently behaving in a way that others can rely on. Booker T. Washington summed it up perfectly when he said, "Character is power." Character is probably the most challenging component because it can strengthen or weaken the other two trust components and requires consistent self-discipline. To get a better understanding of trust, we ought to examine its origin. The Greek word for character, *charassein*, means to engrave or stamp. When something is etched or stamped, it leaves an indelible mark. We demonstrate our character when we keep our word, follow through on our commitments, and respond in ways that help others grow to depend on us.

The unfortunate thing about character is we are taught that it is one-dimensional. For example, if a leader makes a poor decision, she is quickly dismissed as someone who lacks character. Character requires self-discipline. And we all have certain character traits that are stronger than others. You may be strong in honesty but have to work hard at being courageous. It doesn't mean you have "bad" character. It just means you must recognize the barriers that stand in the way of you being more courageous and then be intentional about overcoming them. You may do this at a pace that others feel is too slow.

The second component of trust is connection. It amplifies the need for positive relationships and highlights our ability to influence others. When we focus on relationships, we experience better results, such as more collaboration, higher achievement, and a deeper understanding of others. It requires more work to establish deep connections with others because we are living in the digital age, which often allows for breadth over depth. However, connecting with others is more important than ever.

In a recent post on the *Daily Princetonian*, Kelsey Ji stated the following:

> People are becoming more outcome-oriented when it comes to relationships. Before email was created less than half a century ago, people wrote letters. Letters spanning several pages were written with profound longing emotions and filled with words too embarrassing spoken out loud. Letters that took days and weeks to deliver and even longer to receive a reply. Letters that would be read, reread, mulled over once and again, kept as a charm in the pocket, slept with under the pillow at night. This form of communication, now quite a topic of fascination, was how people of our parents' and grandparents' generations built and maintained connections. Because everything was so slow, perhaps there was only enough time to hold several

dear long-lasting relationships for a lifetime. People knew fewer people and knew them well. People were calmer and happier.

Now? As smartphones became widely available, one's social group not only expanded, but each individual could be reached by pressing one button. With friendships-made-easy social media apps like GroupMe and Instagram that enable no-lag communications and updates across oceans, the process of friend-making is comparable to products on a factory line. And the products that fail to meet production standards are the very people who don't like your photos, who leave you on read, who take too long to respond, etc. As a result, friendships can no longer stand the trial of time.[5]

You are created to connect with others, and lack of human connection leads to many social and emotional issues. You may have experienced this during the pandemic. Isolation has forced us to resort to the more traditional ways of connecting with family and friends while also using technology in innovative ways to experience the connections we so crave.

The third component of trust is competence. Competence describes your ability to do your job with a high degree of fidelity. It's the technical part of your work. You demonstrate competence by consistently removing barriers that prevent teachers from teaching, students from learning, and other school community members from serving. It may be considered the science of leadership. You prove you're trustworthy by sharing information, offering support, and helping your team learn new skills to manage a changing world. The aim is to help others achieve their goals and equip them with the knowledge and trust they need to cope with continuing stresses.

Self-Awareness and Self-Management

Self-awareness is the ability to control and be responsible for what you say and how you behave. It may be easy to blame others or external circumstances for the negative words you spew or the negative way you respond to what you don't like. We all have triggers: people, places, things, events, or words. Being self-aware is having knowledge of what triggers your negative emotions and taking the initiative to develop the skills to respond appropriately. By doing this, you increase the chance that others will trust you. Becoming more self-aware results from developing a growth mindset. This is not just a belief but a list of behaviors.

There comes a time in the life of every leader when you have to take a hard, honest look in the mirror and ask a fundamental question: "If I weren't me, would I want to follow the example I set?" You know yourself better than anybody else. You know your strengths and weaknesses. And with this knowledge of who you are, what you think, and how you live, you can make an honest assessment of your life.

When I became a principal, I wanted to implement some of the ideas that Todd Whitaker shares in his book *What Great Principals Do Differently: Eighteen Things That Matter Most*. In chapter 15, he recommends that the leader communicate expectations at the beginning of each year. The following is a list of expectations I shared with my staff:

- Respect your students, yourself, your colleagues, and the profession.
- Communicate with parents on a regular basis.
- Manage your classroom by being proactive, communicating clear expectations, and being consistent.
- Be present in the moment.
- Be punctual as a sign of respect.
- Be prepared by planning things in advance to prevent poor performance.

- Continue your professional development by trying new things and growing.
- Celebrate progress and honor the achievements of your students.

To be self-aware, you must be reflective. As I think about what I expect from my staff each year, I ask myself if I meet those same expectations. Here are some of the key concepts I focus on, especially during tough or transitional times.

Respect for Others' Time

My former pastor used to say that punctuality is a sign of respect: respect for others' time, talents, and responsibilities. This not only includes arriving on time but ending on time as well. I found myself arriving late to a meeting that I had scheduled! It was disrespectful and gave others permission to arrive late. I was not setting a good example, and my tardiness potentially damaged trust.

Positive Relationships

I have solid relationships with some of my staff, while other relationships need work on my part. At times, I have gotten in the way of establishing a positive relationship because I was quick to speak, slow to hear, or quick to react. In other words, I didn't make time to be present.

I have always felt that I need to interact with my students and parents more. I rely heavily on my strong administrative team. Each member brings a wealth of experience and individual strengths that I tap into on a regular basis. They build and maintain positive relationships with students, staff, and parents. Establishing positive, meaningful, and engaging relationships takes time, yet they are critical to a leader's success when ensuring the mission and vision of the school come to fruition.

Open-Mindedness

Being open to new ideas is critical because education is currently undergoing a significant transformation. Many of our teachers and students have innovative ideas that can make a huge impact on teaching, learning, and the school climate. It's difficult to follow someone if the only response you hear is no. Fresh ideas are percolating among the members of many school communities. It should be a primary goal of the leader to help these ideas become a reality. We demand much of others and must also hold ourselves to the same expectations. We need to get to yes!

One time, a second-year teacher stopped by my office after school and asked if we could talk. The look on her face had me worried, so I welcomed her to have a seat. I thought she was going to share her concerns about student behavior or ask for help to solve a problem. Man, was I was wrong. What she said to me made a lasting impression.

As soon as she started talking, tears streamed down her face, and she apologetically said, "I accepted a position in another district." I swallowed hard because I was utterly shocked. I felt blindsided and immediately started to ask myself where we went wrong—where I went wrong as the principal. She said she needed a change and that she didn't always feel supported or heard. Her comments were difficult to hear, but I appreciated her honesty. I was keenly aware of how I felt and almost became defensive. I paused, reserved judgment, and focused on listening to what she was saying. After she left, I reflected on the comment she made: "I didn't always feel supported or heard."

At that point, I vowed to do everything within my power to prevent this from happening again. One of our goals was for every student, teacher, and parent to have a sense of belonging. It was a lofty goal, yet we took it seriously. Losing that young, promising, and passionate teacher showed me that we needed to do a better job of connecting with our new teachers. We hired seventeen new teachers the following year. Some had no experience, and a few had four to six years of experience.

I decided to meet with them all once a month in an informal setting to simply connect, share, reflect, and learn from each other.

There was no agenda, the teachers didn't have to prepare anything, and they weren't assigned anything to do. We just talked. We first met in our library media center but decided to meet at Panera Bread, which was on our campus, for the rest of the year. It was amazing to hear these teachers' stories, reflective thoughts about their craft, and suggestions on how we could be better. It was wonderful to see how they supported each other.

Not all of them came each month, but it was OK. These gatherings were for them, not me. There was merely an invitation to attend, not a mandate. Most of the time we would go where the conversation took us, but sometimes I would ask a few questions to guide our discussion:

- What is the most successful thing you've done so far?
- How are you taking care of yourself physically?
- What do you do for fun?
- Have we lived up to what we promised you?
- What's one thing we can do differently?
- What are you planning to change in the next semester?

Before we'd conclude our last meeting of the year, I would ask, "Are these meetings helpful?" These are some of the responses I received through the years:

- "I think they are fun. I look forward to them each month."
- "It's good to see and talk with people outside your department. It's good to learn from others."
- "You make us feel like we are important to you."
- "It's good to hear what the other new teachers are thinking."

I appreciated their commitment, time, and honesty. I used this experience to become more aware of how I responded to others, both verbally and nonverbally, which made me a better leader. Through these conversations, we established trust and created a culture of care.

Don't wait for an experience like this to become more self-aware. Ask your team members how they perceive you. Think about your triggers, areas of improvement, and weaknesses. You must consider the experiences people are having instead of the experiences you want them to have. If these experiences don't match up, do what is necessary to bridge the gap.

Servant Leadership

You create connections and positive relationships when you focus on serving others. You serve others by identifying ways to meet their needs, listening to their point of view, and creating boundaries that protect time and space. But remember that you must take care of yourself first to better serve others. Don't focus on others to the detriment of your health and well-being. No one wins in that situation. Servant leadership is about being a doorway, not a doormat.

My last year as a classroom teacher was 2001. One day, as I was greeting students at my classroom door, I saw a student walking slowly toward me with large tears streaming down her cheeks. She was not a student in my class, but I knew her and her family. I greeted her, and she smiled and said, "Hello." Her tone was flat, and she tried to muster up some happiness to avoid a conversation. I asked, "What's wrong?" Instantly, she started sobbing uncontrollably right there in the hallway. I gently took her arm and pulled her toward me, and I asked her to wait by my door because I had to get my class started.

After a few minutes, I walked back to the hallway, and she was still standing there. I asked her where she was supposed to be. Then I walked to her teacher's classroom to let him know she was with me. When I returned, I asked the student if she'd like to talk. We sat down on the floor with our backs against the lockers, and she poured her heart out. I listened attentively, expressed concern, and only offered advice if she asked for it. We talked for a few more minutes, and she finally said, "Can I go home?" I walked back into my classroom. As my students worked quietly on their assignment, I called her school counselor, who then called her parents. I told her to go get the work she had missed from her teacher and then go to the attendance office because her mother was coming to pick her up. The student thanked me for noticing her distress and taking the time to listen.

The next day, I received a call from her mother. She provided more context and expressed her gratitude for my care. The next year, I became an assistant principal in the same building, and I was assigned students whose last names began with A through F. The young lady was not in the alphabet of students I was responsible for! However, I told her parents that I would look after her. We had a few more meaningful conversations.

Her parents became active members of several committees I facilitated, and her father helped launch a mentoring group for young men in the school. He is the epitome of a positive mentor and professional. Her mother is simply a class act, and the student's sister and I were colleagues for over a decade.

Many years after I first helped this student, my wife and I were invited to her wedding. Another time, I ran into her mother while shopping, and she brought up that long-ago conversation! Recently, I joined a Zoom call with a team of educators from another district to discuss their approach to diversity, equity, and inclusion. Guess who was a member of the team? The young lady I spoke to in the hallway in 2001! She is an elementary school teacher in a neighboring school district, and her assistant superintendent sums her up with these words: "She is a rock star!" When you focus on others, you strengthen your connections, and that makes your influence immortal.

Stephanie Rothstein

EdTech TOSA (Teacher on Special Assignment)
Santa Clara Unified School District
San Jose, California

Educator Stephanie Rothstein understands the positive impact of establishing relationships with students. She uses design thinking to connect with her students in a much deeper and more intentional manner. I learned about Stephanie Rothstein while listening to her interview on a podcast called *The Innovator's Mindset.*[6] I was intrigued by her intentionality in using research-based strategies to establish positive relationships with students. She learns about her students in ways that make sense for her classroom design so that establishing positive relationships isn't burdensome.

I have learned a great deal about establishing relationships in my eighteen years as an educator.

Ten years ago, during my first year at my current school, one of my ninth-grade English students at my former school passed away from suicide. This was not a student whom I was worried about in this way. I thought they seemed connected. I realized after this that what I see on the outside does not always match what is going on inside. I knew I needed to do a better job of authentically connecting. This event is what propelled me to take time to build connections, provide opportunities for students to share, and really listen.

To establish relationships, I first need to understand how students would like to have conversations. I find that in my Design Thinking Pathway, we are always asking students to collaborate, but we really need to help them learn how to do this. That is why I started canwetalkedu.com. I use the True Colors personality assessment to help me learn about each student. After taking the survey, students discover which of four colors they are (gold, green, blue, or orange).

The True Colors personality assessment is a research-based assessment that gives you insight into your personality type. It provides information about how you socialize, connect, and collaborate with others, and it helps you increase your self-awareness.

While the survey provides an overview, it does not encompass the entirety of a person. However, it is a great first step to learning how to approach conversations and listen empathetically. I ask students to reflect on what strengths they bring to a team and how they would like to receive feedback and be approached.

I also ask them to record these reflections in Flipgrid. I watch every one of these and respond. Prior to working in a team, students watch the videos of their teammates, which helps establish comfort prior to talking in person or in a breakout space. After I understand how they prefer to have conversations, I listen to the students—really listen. I must provide opportunities for them to share with me and with one another, and I must honor the voices of those in the room. Students must feel safe and know that their voices are honored. Daily check-ins and project topics provide real opportunities for authentic connection.

The biggest challenge of authentic relationship building is time. The best way I have learned to combat this is to ensure that students are a part of relationship-building opportunities. One of the extra projects in my class is to create connection opportunities for other students. Students can work in a smaller group, choose a focus for this project, and connect over it. This year, students created a variety of opportunities: Funny Topic Debate Club, Cooking Club, Mix and Mingle Club, Volunteer Group, and Book Club. I must build in time during class and then use the outside class opportunities to really connect with students on another level.

The suicide and a series of other events made it evident that students needed to share how they were feeling. As a result, my school established a program called CASSY (Counseling & Support Services for Youth). It provides counselors who specifically focus on mental health and support. The program allows me as the teacher to recommend a specific counselor if a student shows any warning signs.

Without a doubt, mental health issues have become a greater priority during my educational career. Each year, I attend more and more training sessions to help me better understand what students may be dealing with. I find we have more and more support groups and opportunities. Our district surveys continue to reveal that students are experiencing mental health issues.

It is important that we educators model the practices we want to see. If we want to help students build relationships with us and one another, we need to model this practice with the staff around us. Whatever we ask of students, we must be willing to do ourselves. It is not my job to fix anything that a student shares with me. They don't need fixing; they need people who can listen to and support them. As educators, we must ensure that we are all trained to provide this support. Building relationships takes time, but it is important, and the effort and energy you put in will enhance the work produced in your classroom.

I admire Stephanie's initiative in responding to the loss of a student. She didn't wait for an administrator or committee to take action. Instead, she focused on what she controlled: her attitude and actions. It was a Maurice Cheeks moment.

Active Listening

Another way to strengthen connections with others is to be an active listener. In the Information Age, we consume thousands of bits of information, from images and written text to videos and voice recordings. We are bombarded with content—so much so that our attention span is extremely short. Author and education consultant Mark White wrote, "Today's attention span is eight seconds on average. Eight seconds. That doesn't mean students won't tune in longer. Clearly, many of them will play video games or text their friends for hours. The eight-second attention span simply means that all of us are making snap decisions about whether your content is worth our time."[7]

When you make snap judgments, you are not as attentive as you should be. You quickly jump to conclusions, make assumptions, and give unsolicited correction and direction. This type of behavior can lead to resentment, which destroys connection. To be an active listener, you can begin by putting down your phone or device and being present with those you are talking to. If culturally appropriate, make eye contact, provide verbal and, more importantly, nonverbal feedback, and ask clarifying questions. If you're connecting via a screen instead of in person, the same rule applies: active listening leads to greater understanding, empathy, and respect.

This reminds me of Jason Headley's video called "It's Not about the Nail."[8] A couple is sitting on the couch, and the woman is describing the aches and pains she's having while the man sits staring at her. After she shares her anguish and confusion about what is causing the pain in her forehead, the man looks sheepishly at her and says, "Maybe it's the nail in your head." Frustrated, the woman replies, "It's *not* about the nail!" Perplexed, the man advises that she will no longer experience the pain or snags in her sweaters if she simply takes out the nail. She slams her hand on the couch and repeats, "It's not about the nail."

The man concedes and continues to listen. The woman proceeds to express her anguish, and she thanks him for listening. When they go in for a kiss, they bump foreheads. The woman grunts in pain, and as the man starts to tell her to remove the nail, she holds up her finger and yells, "Stop!" The moral of the story is that active listening is not about giving unsolicited correction, direction, or advice. It's about hearing the other person's concerns and expressing empathy. We often listen to respond or correct as opposed to understand. The more we understand others' perspectives, the greater our connections will be.

Diversity

To strengthen connections, you must also welcome diversity. You may initially think of identity diversity, which is about race and ethnicity. Being open to the experiences of others from different races, ethnicities, and cultural backgrounds helps you to have a much broader perspective on the people you serve and the type of learning environment you envision. It helps you create the conditions for all students and staff to learn, and it fosters a stronger school community.

As our schools become more diverse, this is more important than ever. You must continue to examine your data: student progress and achievement, attendance and retention, student discipline, and access to a variety of course offerings, extracurricular activities, and experiences. Then you must work with students, staff, and parents to identify and remove barriers so your school lives up to your mission statement.

You must also welcome and affirm cognitive diversity: interests, thoughts, ideas, perspectives, and personalities. Being open to opposing views helps you make others feel seen, heard, valued, respected, and like they belong. You also open yourself to opportunities to think critically about important issues, challenging your assumptions and beliefs so you can grow. You don't have to agree with all perspectives, but connecting with others strengthens trust. Ava DuVernay, director of the movie *Selma*, provided clarity regarding the important work of embracing diversity when she said, "When we're talking about diversity, it's not a box to check. It is a reality that should be deeply felt and held and valued by all of us."[9]

When considering diversity, evaluate who is included in making decisions for the good of all, whose voices are being heard or ignored, whose interests are being served or not, and whose experiences are accounted for. One thing we can do to welcome diversity is to examine our social identity.

Dr. Henri Tajfel developed social identity theory in 1979. In an article summarizing Tajfel's theory, Dr. Saul McLeod wrote, "Social identity is a person's sense of who they are based on their group membership(s)." He continued, "Groups give us a sense of social identity: a sense of belonging to the social world. We divided the world into 'them' and 'us' based through a process of social categorization."[10] Take a moment to think about your friend group, professional network, and the people with whom you spend the most time. How diverse are these groups? Do the people in your groups broaden or narrow your perspective?

The better you understand the groups you may be a part of, either consciously or unconsciously, the better you are at welcoming diversity and being more socially aware. In response to the racial and social unrest in 2020, my district partnered with Dr. Nicole Nieto from The Ohio State University. The goals were to be more responsive to students, to take a deeper look at our diversity, and to unpack our own social identity. She introduced us to the University of Michigan's Program on Intergroup Relations and the Spectrum Center's Social Identity Wheel. This wheel is divided into several identity categories and some reflective questions to respond to.[11] The following groups make up our social identity (in no particular order):

- Race
- Ethnicity
- Gender
- Sex
- Sexual orientation
- Age

- National origin
- First language
- Physical, emotional, developmental (dis)ability
- Religious or spiritual affiliation

When you consider your social identity, you must ask yourself these questions:

- Which identities do I think about most often?
- Which identities do I think about least often?
- Which identities would I like to learn more about?
- Which identities have the strongest effect on how I perceive myself?
- Which identities have the greatest effect on how others perceive me?

Considering these questions was an enlightening exercise because it provided insight on how I see the world and how I see myself. Dr. Nieto and I had some thought-provoking discussions and felt some discomfort due to the cognitive examination. It's important that you examine your social identity and the identity of others without judgment, superiority, or inferiority. It's information that will aid you in finding ways to help others feel welcomed, seen, heard, valued, and respected. This information will also help you to become cognizant of micro-messages that may be a barrier for others. As employee relations expert and attorney DeDe Wilburn Church wrote, "Micro-messages are the small, subtle messages we send and receive verbally and non-verbally. They are mostly unintentional. Through them, we communicate values and expectations subconsciously."[12] You want to be cognizant of your micro-messages because that behavior can hurt relationships and be a barrier to diversity. Because you care deeply about connecting with others, focus on how your attitude and actions are invitations to connect with others, not impediments to connecting with others.

Diane Campbell

Principal Coach
Columbus City Schools
Columbus, Ohio

Diane Campbell is one of those people who doesn't say a whole lot, but when she speaks, people stop and listen. She is reflective and all about action. She is one of the humblest people I know. She cares deeply about family and considers her students and those she serves a part of hers. She recognized that her students and their families had several needs, and she took deliberate steps to create a network of community support to expand services to her students. She created access points and provided opportunities for students to learn from community members. More importantly, she provided opportunities for community members to learn more about her students.

During my almost thirty years in education, expectations for the relationship between schools and community/business partners have drastically evolved. I've always felt that establishing a partnership with community organizations and businesses is important and beneficial to my students and the school.

As a teacher, I often sought out and connected with organizations in the community: recreation centers for after-school support, agencies for financial support, food banks, and so on. I reached out to businesses for financial support and resource donations for school events. During my teaching career, these were mainly one-way relationships.

When I stepped into my school leadership role, I began to see the real meaning and importance of establishing two-way relationships. These are partnerships. I feel the community and businesses have a responsibility to schools because schools are developing future citizens. I believe my school is part of the community. I made it my mission to bring the community and businesses into my school to help establish a partnership in learning. The school can serve the community and businesses if there is such a partnership.

I invited community members and neighboring businesses to join our Site Based Council. I involved them in the planning of school events and created opportunities for students to volunteer at events hosted by community organizations. During my personal time, I attended community-held meetings in the surrounding areas to support various organizations' missions.

It was my mission to expose students and families to as many opportunities as I could, with resource fairs in the evening, business-led workshops for parents during the school day, ESL parent classes during the school day, and so on.

I have to be honest. Establishing a culture where the community and businesses are school partners is exhausting. I spent many evenings and weekends attending events and meetings, returning emails, and calling so many people. I knew I had to be the face of my school to articulate my vision because it was not what the community and businesses were used to.

In my last middle school leadership role, I spent the first year or two saying yes to almost everything that I felt would expose students and families to more opportunities. Exposure changes expectations, and I wanted to make sure students had high expectations for themselves, their community, and their families.

One of the biggest challenges early on was that I was building partnerships and opportunities faster than I was building the internal support I needed to help me manage them.

Over time, I became known for building strong partnerships that positively impacted students and families, so I was no longer exhausting myself seeking out partners; they were coming to us.

I also became more intentional and efficient at investing in our partnerships. Instead of holding and attending separate meetings with community and business partners, I established a monthly roundtable group composed of parents and students, the principal of our neighboring elementary school, and representatives from our community and local businesses. In my last year as the building principal, I added members from the other three area middle schools.

I found ways for my student ambassadors (student leadership team) and my Parent Advisory Council to seek out partnerships with community and business organizations based on what they felt our needs were.

As a teacher, district leader, and school leader, I've always valued relationships. I am intentional about letting people know how important they are and what impact they can have on students and families. I pride myself on knowing that any student, parent, community member, business partner, organization member, or colleague who happens to hear my name feels they were respected by me. Someone saying they built a partnership isn't as powerful as someone showing evidence of how their partnership benefited all parties. Internal partnerships are just as important, if not more important, than external relationships. I've worked hard in every position I've been in to build a trusting partnership with those that I work with so we can establish a level of respect. After all, we are always working toward the same goal.

Be GREAT Tips on How to Be Relational

Being relational is an ongoing process that requires intentionality. As you create connections with others, do not neglect yourself. If you take care of yourself, you will have the capacity, energy, and will to serve others.

To respect the diversity of other thoughts, ideas, and opinions, ask more questions and listen to understand instead of listening to respond.

Spend more time understanding yourself and engage more deeply in conversations. To be more relational, take the following actions:

- Maintain positive relationships with friends outside of school.
- Accept and extend invitations to events.
- Listen out of curiosity, not to critique.
- Remember important dates.
- Celebrate others.
- Work on your emotional intelligence.
- Accept your flaws and appreciate your strengths.
- Understand that disagreement doesn't mean dislike.

Three Questions for Conversation

1 How are you creating and maintaining positive relationships with others?

2 In what ways do you intentionally welcome diversity in your social circle, your classroom, or your school? What are some examples that you have seen or heard about that you would like to implement?

3 Take the True Colors personality assessment. Consider what the results say about your personality and your communication style. What impact does this have on your role and how you relate to others?

FOUR

BE ENTHUSIASTIC

When you know your why, your what has more impact because you're walking in or towards your purpose.

—Michael Jr.

An enthusiastic person is easy to spot. They are typically full of energy, excitement, and intensity; they are emotionally expressive and outgoing. While a part of that description is true, we have lost the original meaning of *enthusiastic*. It is characterized as being primarily based on emotion. Emotions are like swelling: they go up and down based on an external influence. Enthusiasm is much deeper than emotion. The Greek root of the word is *entheos*, which means "God-inspired, possessed, or within." Inspiration comes from knowing your purpose in all that you do, think, and believe. To be enthusiastic means to know and remember your *why*!

I learned a valuable lesson about purpose while playing my first organized sport when I was eight or nine years old. My fraternal twin brother and I joined a neighborhood fast-pitch softball team named the A's, like the Oakland A's. I was selected to play in the hot box, or third base, and I was good at it! I was agile, fast, and had a strong arm that got the ball from third to first base without hesitation.

Dwayne had it all: good looks, speed, charisma, and athleticism. He was the pitcher, the captain, and one of the best players on the team, if not *the* best. I was shorter than my brother, had awfully crooked teeth, wore thick pop-bottle glasses, and was relatively quiet. Looking back on it now, I adapted my behavior to match how others described me: the quiet, shy twin. The labels we use to describe others most often lead to self-fulfilling prophecies, so we must be careful with our words. Dwayne and I did everything together, dressed alike every day, and looked out for each other. It was rare to see us apart.

I don't remember my team's record, but I remember we earned three spots on the all-star team by the end of the season. As practice ended one late summer day, Coach Ronnie, who was no more than twenty years old, gathered us around home plate to let us know who had made the all-star team. I had little doubt I would make the team because I was pretty good.

The first name he called off was Dwayne—of course! He was our pitcher, captain, and leader. The second name he announced was Lonnie, Coach Ronnie's little brother. To say I wasn't the only one shocked by that is an understatement. Finally, he read the third name: Dwight Young.

Dwight Young? Dwight Young was our first baseman, and he, too, was good. In fact, he was outstanding. However, what about me? Dwayne had made the team, so I should have as well, right? We were inseparable and did everything together. How could this be? Dazed and confused, I looked around, waiting for some explanation, but the practice was over. I began to cry—hard. I threw down my glove and took off running toward my mom's car, devastated. I was crushed and felt like a complete failure. How could *I* not make the team? My attitude sucked.

When my mom and brother got to the car, I expected a warm embrace and consoling words. As my mom approached me, I could tell that I was in for something else. I stood there staring at her through my thick, oversized pop-bottle glasses. She grabbed me by the shirt and said, "Don't you *ever* in your life act like that again! Do you hear me? Don't ever act like that again. I mean it! If you want something bad enough, you better earn it! Do you understand me?" That experience taught me a valuable lesson: participation and performance are not the same thing.

I had participated in all the practices and games. I was competitive and played well enough to start. But the other guys were better. Period. (Well, two of the guys.) They consistently performed at a higher level, they were reliable, and they always produced. Here's another way of looking at it: to participate means to rely on our default behaviors—behaviors that are ingrained and automatic. And unless we have been intentional about learning more effective ways to respond to challenges, our default behaviors may not be our best.

Education is a challenging yet rewarding profession. We are asked to do more with less. We must provide more social and emotional support while teaching more standards, and we must ensure every student receives individualized instruction—all while we adjust to rapid changes in state-mandated testing and growing societal needs. We can go through the motions, believing we are doing what is expected of us. We make it through the day, go to bed, and repeat the process the next day, week, month, and year. It can be easy to simply participate in the profession, or rely on our default behaviors, rather than learn new skills so we can perform at a high level on a consistent basis.

What does it mean to perform at a high level, and why is it important? When I think of a performance, I envision giving maximum effort in an inspired manner that evokes emotion and produces positive results. The performer desires to create a positive experience for others. One who performs in life lives a life of purpose, passion, and progress.

Comedian Michael Jr. has a segment during his shows called "Break Time" in which he sits onstage and engages in a conversation with the audience. There is no script, and he has no idea where the conversation will go. In one video featuring this segment,[1] he starts a conversation with a gentleman named Darryl. It just so happens that Darryl is a choir instructor at a military academy. Michael Jr. jokes about Darryl's deep voice and how intimidated his students must be when he calls their names. He gets the crowd laughing and helps Darryl relax a bit. He asks Darryl to sing a few lines of the song "Amazing Grace."

Darryl takes a breath and starts to sing in a deep, melodious voice. Michael Jr. is impressed, and the audience responds with appreciative applause. Then Michael Jr. changes the context. He says, "Now, I want you to give the version as if your uncle just got out of jail, or you got shot in the back as a kid. I'm just saying, I want to see the hood version. You know which version I'm talking about . . . just to see if that version exists. Let me see what you got." As the audience laughs, Darryl looks up to the ceiling and sings one of the most beautiful versions of the song I have ever heard. The crowd gasps, oohs, and ahs, and Michael Jr. is shocked! When Darryl finishes, the audience erupts in applause and several people rush over to shake his hand or give him a hug. It is truly amazing!

The video exemplifies what it looks and sounds like when we know *why* we are doing something as opposed to only focusing on *what* we are doing. When we forget our why, what we do becomes laborious and how we do it becomes burdensome. The more challenges we face, the easier it may become to forget our purpose and solely focus on what we do and how we do it. This can steal our joy, and it will have a ripple effect of negativity in many areas of our lives, including how we behave in our schools and classrooms.

School officials were ordered to shut down schools in March 2020. Administrators and teachers scrambled to provide instruction, support students' well-being, supply food and other necessities, and adapt to some form of online learning. Educators were valued and treated like heroes for the remainder of that school year. News stories hailed the concerted efforts of the educators who provided lessons and the cafeteria staff who packed up meals for entire families and created a pickup system. Creativity went into high gear to maintain traditional ceremonies such as commencement, prom, and other end-of-the-year celebrations. Many educators felt they were fulfilling their purpose.

Schools provided what they could to continue educating children at home, and parents got a taste of what happens all the time in classrooms across the country. Families and whole communities celebrated educators' efforts as they gained a greater appreciation of what it takes to educate children.

As the 2020–2021 school year began, the narrative changed. Government officials mandated that schools remain closed and provide virtual learning only. Many families became enraged at the prospect of their students sitting in front of a computer for most of a school day. Many called teachers lazy and unwilling to work, but the opposite was true. Some educators took to social media to post about the mental and emotional toll they were experiencing. Media outlets started sharing the narrative that it was a year of loss for students because they weren't learning. There were fears about low standardized test scores and the absence of cocurricular and extracurricular activities wreaking havoc on students' social and emotional well-being.

On top of the global pandemic, America was going through social unrest and what some call a racial reckoning. Again, educators felt helpless because they were not with their students to help them process the events. Students, like many adults, turned to social media to express their emotions, share their stories, and engage in conversation. They were processing the events in real time in a very public manner. While attending classes on Zoom, some students refused to turn on their cameras or unmute their microphones, so many educators felt they were talking into a void day after day. It took a toll. Some began to wonder if they were living their purpose. Doubt crept in, and many started to feel anxious, depressed, and ineffective.

Others, however, thrived. Some educators took the initiative to learn new ways to deliver content and make digital learning relevant. They connected with students who didn't necessarily engage in the physical classroom but flourished in the digital environment. They adjusted to the flexible work schedules, provided timely feedback to students, and found ways to engage with families. Some struggled while others thrived. It made me wonder what was making the difference.

The struggling group may have seen their purpose as what they normally did: teach a whole classroom of students, provide content, establish relationships in person, and assess student work. This is like Darryl's first attempt at singing "Amazing Grace," when he did what he was told and did a fine job. It was well-done and met the request. The thriving group may have seen their purpose as something more significant than what they normally did. Maybe they understood the circumstances they faced. If their why was clear and stronger than their what, they were able to adjust to the changing demands. When you only focus on what you do, the destination is the goal. When you focus on why you do what you do, the process is the goal.

In 2003, when I attended my first Jostens Renaissance National Conference, I was blown away by the passionate, excited, energetic, and purpose-filled educators and students I encountered. From the opening pep rally (the most amazing one I had ever experienced) to the heartwarming closing ceremonies, it was an incredible experience. I returned to my school as a different person. It's rare that a conference can change your life, but this one did it for me.

When I got back home, I thought deeply about my why. More significantly, I started to think about my purpose on this earth. What was I born to do? Where was I supposed to be? I reflected on a statement I'd heard from a man named Richard Parkhouse, affectionately called Park. I had attended Park's session at the conference, and I'd written down something he said several times: "Change lives and impact futures." He was referring to the type of climate and culture we should strive to create in our schools and emphasizing that our work is important to the people we serve. Whether we are teaching, coaching, leading, or communicating, the purpose of every interaction is to change lives and impact futures. I loved Park's statement, but there was something missing.

Every interaction you have with others will impact them either positively or negatively. Every time you enter a room, you change the energy of that room. Every word you speak to others affects them in some way. Therefore, for me, it's not just about changing lives or impacting futures. I want to *positively* change lives and impact futures. This became my purpose, and it changed how I interact with others. It changed how I lead and my perception of myself because this purpose is multidimensional and not regulated by a particular position or title.

Principal Baruti Kafele

Consultant, Author, and Retired Principal
Principal Kafele Consulting (principalkafele.com)
Jersey City, New Jersey

Principal Kafele is one of the most sought-after speakers and consultants in the country and a winner of the Milken Educator Award. His intense, honest, and heart-piercing approach empowers educators to identify their purpose, align their behaviors to their purpose, and do what it takes to help all students reach their full potential. He is grounded in his purpose and captivates audiences from coast to coast. He freely shares what drives him in the work he does.

I became a teacher in 1988. I grew up without my father in my home, which proved to be a challenge for my mother. I struggled through high school, attending four different schools and graduating after five years with a 1.5 GPA. I did little to nothing over the next five years, but then I enrolled at Kean University in New Jersey and graduated summa cum laude. My attitude shifted significantly. Although I did not study education, I gravitated toward it, and two years after finishing undergraduate school, I was in a fifth-grade classroom in Brooklyn, New York. I entered this profession for one reason: to teach and model for my boys what it means to be a man. A huge percentage of Black boys grow up with no man in their home and no Black male teachers in their classrooms. I wanted to fill this void. I became a teacher for this singular reason. This was my professional and personal purpose.

When I became a school principal, my purpose didn't change one iota. I walked into my new school for the same reason. This does not imply that I neglected my girls. I didn't. But I wanted to be a walking standard of a man for my boys—a standard of excellence. This included the eventual creation of my Young Men's Empowerment Program. I woke up in the morning for this program. It was my purpose in full effect. I literally watched my boys evolving into young men.

In 2011, I left my principalship to become a full-time, self-employed education consultant and speaker. I had recently written a book titled *Motivating Black Males to Achieve in School and in Life*—another extension of my purpose. The book was so popular that it kept the contracts rolling in for the next few years. Then I noticed that the calls were slowly but surely decreasing. Not everyone wanted my one topic. They had other needs to be met. If I was going to survive in my new career, I needed to evolve quickly. And I did just that.

Over the next eight years, I developed content that I had not preconceptualized. I started writing books, articles, and blog posts that I had not preconceptualized I would write. I started recording videos that I had not preconceptualized I would record. In other words, I was forced to evolve to survive. The silver lining is that throughout my evolution, I was able to keep Black male empowerment at my core. I had to be strategic in doing so, but I was able to keep my focus as I explored other areas of this important work. And my evolution continues to this day.

The work of an educator is so demanding that it is easy to lose or forget one's purpose. It is normal for me to say to educators, "If you have lost your *way*, it is probably safe to conclude that you have lost your *will*. As a result of losing your way and your will, your passion has become *work*. And now that your passion has become work, you have likely lost, forgotten, or misplaced your *why*." At this juncture, I facilitate a mental and emotional journey back in time for these educators so they can rediscover the reason they decided to teach in the first place. This helps them reconnect with their why and recall the point when they knew definitively that they wanted to teach. We then use this to launch a discussion about reconnecting to our purpose, walking in our purpose, and remaining grounded in our purpose so that we remain in the profession.

You can't do this work at an optimal level if you are not grounded in your purpose. A purpose-driven educator is a very different educator from the one who simply shows up for work. The one who shows up for work is just there to do a job. The one who is driven by purpose is on a different level. This person is driven by a passion, mission, and vision. This person will not rest until a sense of accomplishment is realized. Their energy will be felt throughout the entire school community. As I always say, leaving the house without your why is like going to the airport without your ID: there will be no flying that day. Your why is your wings.

Living and working with purpose doesn't mean you should neglect yourself. Your purpose impacts people—mainly the people you serve. You must move from the island of leadership to the influence of leadership. To do that, it's important to identify the barriers to a purpose-driven life.

Curb Your Ego
(Not Your Enthusiasm)

When you live an incongruent life, meaning your head and heart aren't aligned, you are not being honest with yourself. You live in conflict with your purpose. For example, you may know without a shadow of a doubt that the more feedback you give to students about their performance, the deeper their learning will become. You know that regular communication with students' families improves your relationships with them and increases the likelihood of student success. You know that innovation is much broader than the latest tech gadget or app. However, you neglect to make the changes necessary to address these issues.

You may find yourself holding back or protecting yourself from criticism and complaints. Inadvertently, you maintain the status quo, which creates this relentless tension in the pit of your stomach. The reality is that this type of thinking and behavior is purely ego driven. Ego is defined as one's sense of self-esteem or self-importance.[2] A puffed-up ego can lead to stubbornness, and a shrinking ego can lead to emotional or mental paralysis. What does ego-driven behavior look like? And how is it a barrier to our purpose?

Ego-driven behavior is reactionary behavior. It's couched in negativity and a victim mentality. It's a lack of responsibility, a failure of acceptance, and an inability to control our attitude and actions. We know we are driven by our ego when we do the following:

- We allow false stories about our circumstances, relationships with others, and negative outcomes to stream in our heads with little to no supporting evidence.

- We are easily offended by the smallest disagreement or comment. We come off as overly sensitive to anything that is not in complete agreement with our perception or hope.
- We consistently blame others for our emotional state. In other words, our happiness or sadness is beyond our control, and we are at the mercy of the next disruption in our lives. We see disruptions as distractions that derail us from our purpose.
- We are judgmental, critical, and arrogant. We also fail to extend the grace to others that we expect others to give to us.

A few years ago, I was ego driven, especially at home. I rarely talked about work and got defensive about almost everything. Being a school principal is equally challenging and rewarding. It's challenging because of the number of leadership and management decisions that must be made daily, shifting expectations and demands, and the relentless amount of rapidly exchanged information. It's rewarding because of the countless opportunities to impact lives on a daily, monthly, and yearly basis. I immersed myself in the work. I looked forward to attending sporting events, concerts, plays, awards ceremonies, and the like. However, when I became a father, I struggled internally with wanting to be at multiple school events and also at home with my daughter. I never really found the proper balance. I was living incongruently.

I enjoyed preparing for parent and community events, staff meetings, and professional learning opportunities. I enjoyed discussing the work with my administrative team during our weekly team meetings or informal conversations throughout the day (and night). I especially enjoyed visiting classrooms, and I still regret not creating more time for this. Being a principal is demanding. The job requires a great deal of emotional, mental, and physical stamina. It's also a public position, and in today's world of total transparency and immediate information, nearly every decision is scrutinized and debated via email or on social media. Heck, the same can be said for any position in education.

Professionally, my wife is also somewhat of a public figure. Over the years, several of her clients and coworkers had children in the schools where I was the principal. She was often approached by a client or a coworker and asked about a decision I had made or something that may have occurred at school. I was always aware of this possibility and didn't want to put her in the tough position of responding to such questions. To protect her, I decided I would not talk to her about most of the things that happened at school. I'd talk to a principal friend in another state or to my team—or I'd simply not talk at all. My philosophy was ignorance is bliss. For the most part, this strategy seemed to work.

However, when I left my principalship for a year, I realized that the worst mistake I made was that I didn't share my work with her: the good, the bad, the beautiful, or the ugly. I simply didn't talk about it. I thought I was doing it to protect her from those who clamored for insider information, but it prevented us from connecting over an essential part of my life. My ego got in the way. Since then, I've learned three key lessons about the importance of sharing essential parts of your life with your partner: it creates opportunities for connection, it creates opportunities for compassion, and it improves communication.

According to an article on Reference.com, "About one-third or 30 percent of human life is spent working. The average working week in the United States consists of 40 hours of work. Most people take a few holidays every year. On average, most people spend about 25 to 30 years working. Work forms a major part of adult life, and some people equate happiness with the number of hours spent at the office."[3] That's a lot of time spent creating shared experiences and celebrations, going through trials and disappointments, and making an impact. This world should be shared with your partner because for most of us, our purpose is closely aligned to our work—and so much joy can come from it. As I continue to grow as a father and husband, I am thinking more about my purpose in my personal life.

I catch myself wondering why it's a struggle sometimes to be as enthusiastic or purpose filled in my personal relationships as I am in my professional ones. I wonder if it's because I am more goal oriented and outcome driven when it comes to my work. For example, I may do research, talk to others, and try different strategies to help a student or teacher understand a new concept or to break through a barrier with a colleague. But I will not give that same energy when faced with a conflict or problem at home. I exert so much effort throughout the day to be the best version of myself that maybe I only have a little in the tank to give at home. If I only see my purpose aligned to my work, there will be problems at home. Can you relate?

I was trained, either by default, observation, or chance, to believe that my purpose as a husband and father is to provide for my family. In my early life, I was also trained to provide spiritual leadership. I didn't grow up with a father in my home, but I had some outstanding father-figure mentors, including several of my childhood friends' fathers. These gentlemen were hardworking blue-collar men who consistently provided for their families. But I don't remember ever seeing them hugging or kissing their spouses or children. It doesn't mean it didn't happen; it just means I wasn't around when it did.

My grandfathers, Earnest Carter and George Burton, were also hardworking men who sacrificed much to provide for our family. We'd go fishing or take camping trips in Grandpa Burton's RV. Our trips were simple but so much fun! I don't remember their affectionate side. They showed love in different ways, mainly by ensuring our family's needs were met.

I played little league sports as a child and was a collegiate athlete when I was older. Throughout those years, I had several coaches, and I picked up quality characteristics from them that shaped me into the person I am today. These male and female coaches had a desire to help the players on their teams develop as people, and they used the sports they coached to achieve this goal. As I reflect on their influence,

I realize that there were parts of their lives I didn't see—the parts that I may struggle with myself.

My father did the best he could, and as a middle-aged man now, I have a much better understanding of the man he was. However, as a teenager and young adult, I held on to so much anger and resentment. To say that this has impacted me or been a driving force behind my purpose as an educator would be an understatement.

Manage Your Distractions

"Dwight is connected all over the world through Twitter and blogging, but he is not as connected here." One of my veteran teachers made this comment, and man, did it sting. There were several ways I could have reacted to this, but I decided to look within. After all, reflection is at the heart of our practice.

Distractions prevent us from focusing on the most important aspect of our work: the people we serve. Distractions abound, and in the ambiguous and complex work of education, we can easily lose sight of this most important factor. According to author and leadership expert Robert I. Sutton, the author of *Good Boss, Bad Boss: How to Be the Best . . . and Learn from the Worst*, "Research by Gloria Mark and her colleagues shows that it takes people an average of twenty-five minutes to recover from an interruption and return to the task they had been working on—which happens because interruptions destroy their train of thought and divert attention to other tasks."[4]

Imagine checking email, Facebook, Twitter, Instagram, or TikTok several times a day. You could lose up to three or four hours of quality time that could be spent on tasks or collaborating with the people you serve.

I asked myself if there was any kernel of truth to the veteran teacher's comment. I had begun to relish the connections I was making across the country. I had become so focused on telling stories on Twitter about what was happening at our school that I didn't spend as much time on face-to-face interactions with my staff. I no longer consistently walked the halls throughout the day. I felt myself becoming increasingly impatient with small talk, and I was no longer willing to be inconvenienced. I was quickly irritated, overly sensitive, and less talkative. I started to dislike how I was doing my job. My ego was driving my behavior, and my actions weren't aligned with my words.

I made a deliberate effort to put away my phone when I spoke with others throughout the day. I also put it away when I got home so I could just relax with my family. And I stopped blogging for a while. These actions enabled me to reconnect with others who were physically present. I had to reconnect intentionally and purposely not just for them—but for me. Sutton wrote, "Listen to those under your supervision. Really listen. Don't act as if you're listening and let it go in one ear and out the other. Faking it is worse than not doing it at all."[5] Thankfully, I was surrounded by people who told me the truth, and I set my ego aside long enough to listen.

I absolutely love being an educational leader. I love it when my colleagues and I overcome challenges together. I love talking with members of my staff about their lives, and I love spending quality time with my family. And yes, I love positively promoting my school district through social media, but it only matters if the people I serve feel that I am emotionally connected and present with them every step of the way.

Cultivate Clarity

Clarity in communication is everything. One time, when I was excitedly presenting new information to my staff about some key changes and ideas for improvement, I forgot some important guidelines that would have alleviated stress and prevented feelings of frustration. Here they are:

- Clearly and succinctly state the purpose. Many people are open to new ideas, but knowing the purpose of them helps with buy-in and can increase the number of supporters of the change.
- Clearly and succinctly state what is changing. Many people simply want to know what you, the leader, expect from them so that they can meet expectations. If clearly presented and shared properly, *your* expectations will easily become *their* expectations.
- Clearly and succinctly state how things are going to change. While it is difficult to outline every aspect of this, it's important to provide a road map even though it will evolve as you engage members in conversation and gather feedback.
- Clearly and succinctly state when the changes will occur. It is impossible to have all the answers. However, providing a flexible time line will allow dialogue, training, and implementation.
- Provide adequate time for questions, conversation, and resources. If the change is significant, you must provide data to support why you want the change to occur and provide a channel for dialogue to take place. Additionally, you must ask yourself some key questions:
  - Will this help us fulfill our mission and vision?
  - Is this what's best for all students? How do we know?
  - Will this help us accomplish our specific goals as a school?
  - Is this in line with our values as a school?

Whether we are talking to students, teachers, parents, the board of education, or community members, we not only have to focus on *what* we present but also *how* we present it.

Conquer Incompetence

Incompetence is a barrier to living a purpose-filled life when it causes paralysis. Because being an educator is nuanced, complex, and requires calculated risk taking, experiencing incompetence is normal. Ask yourself, as you reflect on your work, what *your* level of incompetence is.

Robert I. Sutton defines incompetence as "one's inability to complete a task due to a lack of knowledge and/or skill."[6] To admit your own level of incompetence is frightening but also liberating. It's showing vulnerability. I choose the term *frightening* because as a leader, you are looked to for direction, insight, and guidance. At the same time, admitting incompetence is liberating because it opens up opportunities for others to emerge as leaders, empowers others in your organization, and allows for positive changes to take place. And, for me, this aligns with my purpose.

I felt I had reached my threshold of incompetence when it came to taking our building to the next level. I had been a part of some significant changes that challenged our current system so much that I felt we were in a constant state of flux, which was uncomfortable. It often felt like we had two systems battling for supremacy with no idea which one would win—or if there even should be a winner.

I couldn't shake the feeling of chaos. Was I feeling incompetent or uncomfortable? When you face a challenge, do you feel uncomfortable or incompetent? I bet the answer is that you feel uncomfortable. This is because your normal paradigm has been shaken and you are forced to learn new ways of thinking and develop different strategies to convey a compelling message to lead others to change. Isn't that what learning is all about?

Inspire Creativity

When we are certain of our purpose, there is more room for creativity, collaboration, and clarity. However, when we experience a lack of creativity, we lose sight of our purpose again. Creativity can be expressed via many outlets, such as blogging, designing, making art, and listening to or making music. According to Laurie Bennett, a founding partner of an organization called Within People, "Purpose supports creativity by giving us meaning. It makes what we do matter, and it means the things we make matter, too. When held proudly, it attracts the people with a passion for what we stand for—clients and colleagues alike—who will create with us."[7]

I've attended the Jostens Renaissance National Conference many times, and each year I walk away feeling inspired and enthused about my purpose as an educator. The keynote, featured presenters, and breakout sessions always leave the attendees excited to implement something new in their classrooms, schools, or communities. What's unique about this conference is that about 30 percent of the attendees are students! Students who attend are either formal or informal leaders at their schools. They are just as engaged as all the educators and bring a certain level of energy that is contagious.

One year, I attended the conference and met one of the most creative educators I know. His name is Kevin Honeycutt, and he is an expert on meaningful learning. He shared several tidbits of information that piqued my interest. His presentation was creatively engaging and stressed how we can harness the power of technology and relationships to make learning more meaningful for ourselves and for our students.

We are all creative. We simply need the freedom to put a creative idea into action, reflect on the results, and try again. Laurie Bennett, continuing to explain the importance of creativity, stated, "Creativity in flow is a blissful, mindful, mindless state. But creativity can also be a spawning ground for fear, insecurity, paralysis."[8] It's easy to criticize what's new, and it takes courage to embrace, support, and enthusiastically share what risk takers are doing. You must protect them from the naysayers by publicly recognizing, rewarding, and reinforcing their behavior. Additionally, you need to protect yourself so that you can continue to take calculated risks. The result will be more risk-taking behavior by others and more alignment to your purpose.

Learning sticks when you connect content and experience to emotion. My favorite educators I have worked with are the ones who make learning meaningful through emotional connections. This might involve song, performance, meaningful projects, creating a supportive and collaborative classroom environment, and setting high expectations. Students respond by being committed to the learning process, working hard for the teacher, and removing any walls that would prevent learning. They stay after school and work together on weekends to solve problems, complete quality projects, or perfect a performance. It's amazing to see! According to writer, educator, and self-proclaimed neuroscience nerd Trynia Kaufman, "If you have a supportive principal who has established psychological safety in your school, you might be more likely to challenge yourself and try new ideas in your classroom. But if school leaders consistently give critical feedback, you might not feel psychologically safe enough to try something new. It's the same for students."[9]

Mandates, accountability, and standardization squelch creativity. Standards are necessary and should be followed. They protect students and educators by providing boundaries that can guide innovation. However, you must break through these mandated and oftentimes self-made barriers to be remarkable at your craft. You are creative in your own ways, and the more you foster creativity in your classroom and school, the more you will help students love learning. You can even make learning as exciting for them as it was during their primary school years. This is the type of culture you ought to strive for.

The ability to perform under pressure not only sparks creative problem solving but also opens up more opportunities for personal growth and helping others. I tend to take myself way too seriously, and it's during these times that I am less creative, less effective, and almost paralyzed with insecurity. I must remember to refocus on my purpose, let go, and just do. Remembering our why helps us develop the resilience we need to make an impact on our students and communities.

Pathway to Purpose

Defining what it means to have a "successful" school is quite the challenge, with stakeholders often disagreeing on the approach to take. Some primarily focus on what's easily quantifiable, such as standardized tests, attendance data, GPAs, and discipline data. While these data points are important, they don't always tell the whole story or clearly define the success of a school.

Salome Thomas-EL, Ed.D

Principal, Speaker, and Author
Thomas Edison Public Charter School
Wilmington, Delaware

Dr. Thomas-EL is a passionate school leader who does whatever it takes to provide opportunities for his students. His mantra is "I Choose to Stay" because he believes he has more work to do to help each student reach their full potential. It's his purpose.

My work has been aligned with my purpose in life for years. I have been enthusiastic and passionate about providing equal and robust educational opportunities for all my students. Over my twenty years as a school leader, I have sought to develop school cultures that lift others through positivity, allow adults and students to build powerful relationships, and create a supportive environment. I wake up each day with the determination to be more equity focused and trauma informed as a teacher and leader.

Early in my career, when I was a teacher in the inner city of Philadelphia, I realized there were persistent achievement and opportunity gaps among the students I served, and the students in suburban communities were more advantaged. I knew that I needed to find a way to close those gaps and create opportunities for my students to become resilient and persistent and find success in school and life. I began to focus on developing effective after-school and Saturday school programs that taught students to think critically, problem solve, and advocate for themselves.

As a fairly new K–5 principal, I realized our students were struggling in middle school (academically and behaviorally). There were honor roll students in elementary school who were not finding success in middle school. I knew that they'd had great relationships with their teachers in elementary school and were probably struggling with trusting others and establishing new connections. Students in high-poverty and distressed communities often find it difficult to trust adults and develop new relationships.

Also, through research, I learned that middle school students in K–8 schools had better grades, higher attendance rates, and fewer discipline occurrences. I decided to convert my school to a K–8 elementary and middle school building. I made these plans but did not fully realize my staff's concerns about having older students in our school. We knew it was best for the students, but it took careful planning and plenty of professional development for our teachers, administrators, and parents. After learning to listen to my staff more and seek out their input and expertise, we successfully developed an award-winning K–8 inner-city school. During this process, I learned the importance of student engagement and how it is impacted by developing social-emotional skills, teacher influence, and positive relationships.

Many educators may forget their purpose or lose their way over the years, but this is a journey, and we can find our passion again. I often tell teachers and leaders that they are tired but also uninspired! I try to remind educators to think about what led them to the profession and what keeps them in the fight for our students. The positive and stable relationships we establish with kids help them to overcome adversity and trauma. When we show them empathy, caring, and love, we can offer them a feeling of safety and security that they may struggle to find at home or in the community. Connecting with other teachers and leaders on social media can be a great way to find mentors and others who share the same passion for our profession. Educators should find places to work where they are celebrated and not just tolerated.

As I matured as a leader and my purpose began to crystallize, I wanted to take a much broader approach to defining the success of the schools I lead. I wanted to intentionally focus on the development of the whole child. Following, I've outlined seven attributes (or seven A's) I consider essential in a high school, as well as my rationale for selecting them.

- **Attendance:** Students must be in school and be on time every period, every day. They must also be present mentally. Presence matters, and it is an easily identifiable characteristic of successful schools. It's a skill necessary for success in life, and by making it a priority, students develop the habit of showing up regardless of their chosen path: postsecondary enrollment, enlistment in the armed forces, entrepreneurship, or full-time employment. Purpose-driven educators create an environment where students want to attend and be engaged every day. For example, create multiple ways for them to have their names in lights: announcements, acknowledgments in the local newspaper, digital monitors displaying their pictures throughout the building, or social media posts celebrating positive behavior. Find inexpensive and creative ways to recognize progress and achievement.

- **Academics:** Schools that offer a variety of relevant courses meet the needs of students while also encouraging them to experiment with unfamiliar content. Students can learn by doing and solve local, state, national, and global problems in creative ways. This provides opportunities for teachers to connect with other educators beyond the school walls and model the collaborative learning process. I recommend that a school review its program of studies annually to ensure it's providing the best opportunities for students. One of the most important things a principal can do is support the development of new courses that meet the needs of today's learners. Support teachers who create classes that tap into students' passions.

- **Attitude:** It's important that school leaders create a culture that celebrates positive attitudes in students, staff, and parents. One's attitude is reflected in one's behavior—and it's contagious. It's better to spread positivity than negativity. Creating a culture of responding appropriately to setbacks (such as by viewing them as learning opportunities) leads to a much more pleasant environment and a sense of belonging.

- **Acts of Service:** Community service is the norm in successful schools, and it doesn't always have to take the form of large one-time events. Classes or entire grade levels can partner with local organizations such as the Ronald McDonald House Charities, a local food bank, an animal shelter, the American Red Cross, and nursing homes, or they can assist neighbors with home projects. The possibilities are endless if there is a plan and a desire to help others. This not only creates a sense of belonging for students who have the heart to serve others but also establishes solid school-community partnerships.

- **Athletics:** A solid athletics program provides an outlet for students, creates opportunities for them to connect with each other over a common interest, and gives them the focus they may need to perform academically. In addition, athletics foster positive relationships and increase school pride because the school community rallies around the teams that are in-season, providing weekly opportunities to celebrate them and the school.

- **Arts:** A robust performing and visual arts program gives students the opportunity to stretch themselves, fulfill a passion, perform in front of audiences, and immerse themselves in creative outlets. The arts showcase the talent that exists within a school, and the community will gather to see students in action.

- **Activities:** Successful schools have a number of clubs and extracurricular activities, such as a gamers' club, e-sports, a robotics team, table tennis, a Japanese anime club, a programming club, a chess club, or a writers' club for students who express themselves through poetry and the written word. It's important to honor students' voices by allowing them to decide which clubs they want to have at school. The only stipulation is that a school employee must agree to be the club adviser. Use school announcements, social media, and other tools to share meeting times and dates as well as highlights from club meetings.

Focusing on the seven A's will lead to an overall successful school by giving every student the opportunity to thrive. The seven A's encompass areas that appeal to all stakeholders, so everyone can find their niche and be a part of building a positive school culture. As a final step, track data and share results with students, staff, parents, and the community to ensure buy-in and continued school success.

Be GREAT Tips on How to Be Enthusiastic

Enthusiasm is less about the outward expression of emotion and more about your purpose. Revisit your why by remembering the reasons you chose this job and reflecting on how you choose to show up each day. Consider how you can best serve students, colleagues, families, and your own family. Your purpose is multidimensional, just as you are. Focus on finding ways to live your purpose apart from your profession because your profession is just one reason why you do what you do. Take that away, and you still have a purpose. Never be too busy to live your purpose, or you will become worn out. What good does that do you or anyone else? To be more enthusiastic, try the following:

- Focus on why more than how or what.
- Develop goals aligned to your purpose that are not necessarily what others want from you.
- Cultivate a practice of gratitude.
- Be intentional about selecting a diverse group of mentors with different interests and expertise.
- Develop a growth mindset.

Three Questions for Conversation

1 What is your purpose, and how is it exemplified in the experiences you create for others?

2 When you forget your purpose, what does that look like and how do you rediscover it?

3 How do you expand your influence and impact others with your life and your energy?

FIVE

BE AUTHENTIC

Maybe the journey isn't so much about becoming anything. Maybe it's about unbecoming everything that isn't really you, so you can be who you were meant to be in the first place.

—Paulo Coelho

According to Dictionary.com, to be authentic means to be true to one's own personality, spirit, and character.[1] As I've evolved and learned, I've come to realize that I define authenticity as a journey to learn about yourself—your character strengths, triggers, weaknesses, boundaries, and aspirations—so that your head and heart are aligned. My journey to be authentic began after a painful event.

In 1999–2000, after a failed marriage, I experienced my first battle with depression. We both had high expectations of ourselves and were goal oriented. We were great friends, so out of sheer stubbornness we forged ahead to the altar despite disapproval from both our families and significant red flags. We knew we had made a mistake within a few months and finally decided to end it after less than a year. It was devastating in several ways.

My *perception* was that I had failed morally and socially. I had a difficult time accepting responsibility for my negative attitude during the marriage, which impacted my actions—or lack thereof. I had a victim's mentality. The failure to take responsibility for my attitude and actions delayed my healing. I isolated myself from many friends and my immediate family. The vicious cycle of negative thoughts, shame, and embarrassment caused me to implode. As I look back on that period in my life, how I felt about the situation determined how I behaved toward myself and others.

I wasn't the best teacher during that time, either. I assigned lots of busywork to avoid falling apart in class. I limited class discussions— something that my students and I had enjoyed. Because of the rapport I had with my students, they knew something was wrong. They recognized the changes and responded with love and kindness. A student named Lauren went on a trip to Italy with her father during spring break, and she brought back a gift for me. It was a leather-bound journal with an old-world map on the cover. The message she and her father had inscribed on the inside of the journal let me know just how much my students cared about me.

> Mr. Carter, Hey! We got this when we were in Italy. It's not much, but we thought you might like it. We know you've been going through some rough stuff lately, we don't know what though. But, we hope you get better and remember that "any day above ground is a GOOD DAY!" As you always tell us! PS: We figured that you could write the important stuff in here.

It was a sweet gesture that provided hope and reassured me that while I saw myself as a failure, my students didn't see me that way. When your identity is wrapped up in how you want others to see you, any deviation from that can cause serious emotional pain and mental anguish.

I met with a therapist for nearly six months, took an antidepressant, journaled, and started to exercise again. I began to feel better as I opened up to a few close friends and mentors. Several heroes emerged to help me. One was a coworker and dear friend named Justin Hammond. We coached track together and talked every day. He saw me physically getting weaker and offered to help. He didn't nag or force, but he supported and worked with me to create a plan to get healthier. We worked out together during our planning period.

There was a network of support around me. My principal and two teaching colleagues met with me every day to check in and talk about life. My pastor and his family provided comfort and companionship by inviting me to dine with them, attend baseball games, and just hang out. I turned away from my immediate family out of sheer shame and because I believed I was a failure in their eyes, which was the most ridiculous and false narrative I fed myself. They hurt because I hurt, and I hurt them more because I didn't let them in. My feelings still dictated my behavior. I did what I thought I was supposed to do to appear normal. I didn't profoundly and authentically lean into my reality. I rushed through the healing process. I probably quit therapy too soon. I stopped my medication because I began to feel much better and didn't want my mind altered by a synthetic substance. I tried to will myself to better health because others' perceptions of me were more important than me showing up as my authentic self. Heck, I'm not sure I even knew who that was.

I started feeling successful at school again and was excelling in my classes to get my master's degree. I was doing fine. As I reflected on my life, having a better understanding of chronic depression, I saw that I needed the medication to correct the chemical imbalance in my brain.

I needed it to think more clearly. The only way I would become healthy was to change my behavior and attitude. Researcher and author Dr. Brené Brown wrote, "We don't change, we don't grow, and we don't move forward without the work."[2] I was doing the work but continued to struggle a bit. I didn't know it then, but what I felt most was shame. Dr. Brené Brown also wrote, "I define shame as the intensely painful feeling or experience of believing that we are flawed and therefore unworthy of love and belonging—something we've experienced, done, or failed to do makes us unworthy of connection. I don't believe shame is helpful or productive. In fact, I think shame is much more likely to be the source of destructive, hurtful behavior than the solution or cure. I think the fear of disconnection can make us dangerous."[3]

My foundation as an educator rested on the cornerstone of positive relationships, and I believed I had failed at one of the most important relationships we can have with another person. I felt like a hypocrite and thought it reflected poorly on me personally and professionally. I wanted nothing more than to feel whole again. I was afraid to be authentic. I don't think I knew who I was at the time, which is why the pain was so deep. I was who I thought everyone wanted me to be.

In chapter 4, I shared how others' perceptions of me influenced my behavior, creating a self-fulfilling prophecy. Because I wore glasses and was less outgoing than my brother, I was called the shy, quiet, and smart twin—so that's how I acted. While those characteristics were positive and admirable, I learned to suppress or deny any part of me that didn't fit that perception. It all came to head in 1999 because I was living an incongruent life: my head and heart were not aligned.

I felt like my most authentic self in the classroom, on the field as an assistant football coach, or on the track as an assistant track coach. I was at my happiest in those moments because I was not only doing what I loved—I felt like I had a purpose, meaning, and drive. I could see that I was making a difference. I experienced joy in helping young people achieve their goals and aspirations, and I was working with a team of educators invested in students' lives.

Students today are demanding space and opportunities to be their authentic selves. They use their collective voice to share their ideas about how to create schools they want to experience rather than merely attend. In their lifetime, they have experienced two economic recessions; they have led national and global protests on gun violence in schools, climate change, and racial and social injustice; and they have endured a global pandemic that exposed them to other ways of experiencing school—some good and some bad. They are aching for authenticity and will not settle for conditions that prevent it. Many of them use social media platforms to showcase their musical, artistic, scientific, and other creative talents. They are not afraid to talk with their teachers and administrators about the curriculum, supplementary teaching materials, and resources that reflect a diverse community. They want and expect to see themselves throughout the curriculum, and they want to learn about other cultures. As they embrace their authenticity, they also want to celebrate the diversity they have grown up with.

Student Beans, a global marketing and technology company, surveyed Generation Z students (born between 1997 and 2012) to get insight on their values, ethics, and beliefs. A 2020 Student Beans article stated, "95% of Gen Zs the world over have taken action towards a cause that they believe in. Being authentic for Gen Z means speaking your truth and advocating for what you believe in. It's an attitude that's propelled them into positions of activism as part of the Black Lives Matter movement last May, and inspired them to seek careers in climate change. A lot of Gen Z's ethics and values stem from a common theme—everyone should be free to be their authentic selves."[4]

An article about authenticity reviewed by *Psychology Today* stated, "We are drawn to genuine people—rather than people who simply agree with whatever we say or do—because those who are true to themselves are also likely to be true and honest with us. Authenticity is also associated with many appealing traits, including confidence, strength, individuality, and emotional resilience."[5] When you cultivate the courage to be authentic and are rewarded for it, you become much more comfortable with being your genuine self. The more comfortable you are, the easier it is, and you establish better relationships with others because you are accepted for who you are. Think of this from another perspective as well. When your students and staff members are trying something new—taking the lead on a project or coming up with a way to solve a long-standing problem—they are vulnerable, and you must recognize and reward the efforts they are making as their authentic selves. When this becomes the norm, everyone benefits. I am a much better colleague, educator, friend, and leader when I show up as my authentic self. When we create psychologically safe school cultures and common goals, values, and standards, students thrive.

Dr. Donja Thomas

English Educator and Black Studies Curriculum Developer
Creator of African American Voice
GLHS Diaspora Cofounder and Adviser
Lincoln High School
Gahanna, Ohio

Dr. Thomas is one of the most intelligent, student-centered, and authentic educators I know. She is the creator of the African American Voice literature course. As an advocate for all students, she has made it her mission to create space for their voices, to develop their self-awareness, and to foster a culture of transparency. She describes how she helps students cultivate the necessary skills to channel their authenticity.

Emphasis on critical thinking and the importance of self-education are vital in my teaching practice. I always make it a point to expose students to relevant materials by writers, authors, historical figures, creatives, and voices with important legacies that are typically not taught in school curricula. I expose them to people overlooked or even silenced due to the power and fearlessness they display when speaking their truth and following their instincts. This showcases to students that they are meant to be agents of change and that their courage is needed to disturb the social oppression that functions in their communities; it is their courage that moves them from victim to conqueror.

I also emphasize that most of the "leaders" they know of today did not title themselves as such. They were just ordinary human beings who found themselves at the right place at the right time and chose to meet the moment. If young people decide to fulfill their moment, that is their contribution. If they decide to stay silent, that is also their contribution. If nobody looks for them, they should look for themselves! They are the ones they have been waiting for to save their lives!

In my classroom, I try to exemplify what I teach by demonstrating that everything I am asking students to do is something I am also willing to do. I tell them they are multifaceted and should not define themselves according to just one strength. I show them that they can be a doctor of philosophy, an educator, a writer, an entrepreneur, etc., all at the same time. I read and annotate everything I assign to them, and I actively unpack it with them to showcase that learning is infinite and a lifelong journey. We can always know more. I try to showcase that (even with a busy life) we will make time to do the things that matter to us, and if we stay ready for the opportunities we seek to attract, we don't have to get prepared.

I tell them that they are writers because they use writing to express their perspectives. I constantly remind them that they have the power to create their definitions of self. I tell them that they are born in and on purpose and that they are uniquely made. They are one of one. When you commit to showing, not just telling, students who they are, they will believe you.

To encourage authenticity in my students, I create an environment conducive to original expression. I may start class off with some form of audio or visual sharing (art, music, film, a news story, TikTok, etc.) tied to a theme of study to get them engaged. Then, instead of taking attendance, I begin class by asking a question that is usually tied to the central theme of that day's lesson. Since everyone is sharing, they don't feel judged, and since I affirm each response, they enjoy sharing their perspectives and stating their opinions while also learning to appreciate their peers' unique voices and responses. They also realize that they can give no wrong answer. Each class, they become more comfortable using their voices without fear of criticism.

Overall, I believe that when students see themselves reflected in their learning, they begin to see themselves as the change agents they were born to be. Their influence becomes actualized among their peers, family, and community through the insights they share, the integrity they display, the bigotry they confront, the knowledge they seek, and the belief in themselves that they cultivate daily as they actively create the reality they want to experience.

Dr. Thomas provides several key takeaways that can be applied in any classroom:

- Make learning relevant by exposing students to a variety of different voices and genres.
- Show students examples of change agents and remind them that they, too, are agents of change right now.
- Remind students that they are multidimensional and have many strengths. Acknowledge their strengths as often as possible.
- Model a growth mindset.

- Be creative in lesson design, instructional strategies, and personal reflection.
- Express ongoing belief in students.

As you think about your work, your students and colleagues, and the people you serve, consider the overall working environment and culture. Does it embrace authenticity or force conformity? Don't get me wrong; there must be clear rules, expectations, and procedures to follow because they create a safe environment to work in. But within the established boundaries, there must be room to function as genuinely as possible so that everyone benefits.

The more you become your authentic self, the more aware you are of what inspires you. So what inspires you? Do you know? Do others know, too? If not, take some time to reflect on that question, jot down what comes to mind, and take action without shame, fear, or guilt.

I'm not oversimplifying the steps toward authenticity. After all, it's a lifetime journey. Some are further along in their journey than others, but we are all right where we need to be. As you think about your role and the people you serve, continue to ask yourself two critical questions:

- How am I creating the conditions for others, especially my students, to be their most authentic selves?
- What do I need to be my most authentic self so that I can better serve others?

In a video called "'Jiggly Boy' Returns . . . and KG Approves: Funny Video 2015,"[6] a fan at a 2003 Minnesota Timberwolves game, in his excitement over Kevin Garnett (KG), starts dancing in the aisle. As the crowd cheers him on, he takes off his blue, black, and white Timberwolves shirt to reveal a gray cutoff T-shirt with the Timberwolves name and logo on the front. As he continues to dance, he shows off the large initials "KG" written on his arm in what looks like black shoe polish. The crowd continues to cheer him on as his image is displayed on the jumbotron. Feeling pretty good about himself, the guy rips open the gray cutoff shirt to reveal "Timberwolves 1" on his chest and belly, and the crowd erupts! He dances and lives his best life! Suddenly, two security guards approach him as he's in the middle of a dance move, and they escort him out of the stadium. He waves to the crowd, embarrassed. He returns with a new team shirt with "15" on it; the mascot runs to his side, and they dance a jig before Jiggly Boy takes his seat. The 2003 segment of the video ends.

Kevin Garnett left the Timberwolves in 2007 to join the Boston Celtics, where he helped them win an NBA championship. He then went on to play for the Brooklyn Nets before returning to the Timberwolves in 2015. Kevin Garnett's return was also the return of Jiggly Boy. If you have ever attended a live sporting event, such as a basketball, baseball, or hockey game, you'll know there's usually a period when a DJ plays music. Simultaneously, the cameras scan the crowd to find people dancing in their seats. These fans are displayed on the jumbotron and, at the Timberwolves arena, they are invited to show off their dance moves.

As the video continues, now in 2015, Jiggly Boy is spotted in the crowd, and the fans cheer, but he is not interested in getting removed from the stadium again, so he humbly rejects the invitation from the announcer to dance. He points to his kids, and they dance a bit.

After a plea from the announcer, the camera pans to a person who waves their hands in the air, then to a person who does a generic fist pump to the beat of the music. Then, the camera pans back to Jiggly Boy, who sheepishly refuses to dance again. He again points to his kids, and they dance a bit. The announcer lets him off the hook, and the camera pans to a person who takes his best shot at pumping up the crowd. The announcer then says, "Let's give it one more try." The camera turns back to Jiggly Boy. At the sound of Lil Jon's "Yeah!" followed by the beat drop, Jiggly Boy steps into the aisle with his two sons as background dancers and goes off! The fans explode with excitement as he breaks out his best moves and rips off the same jersey he was given in 2003 to reveal "Welcome Home, KG" painted on his chest and belly! KG responds with approval, and all is right in the world.

In 2003, Jiggly Boy presented his authentic personality, spirit, and character but was quickly deflated by the security guards who ushered him out of the stadium. The message was that he was too much for them, his ideas were silly, and his actions weren't acceptable. His efforts didn't fit in, and he needed to be tamed. Like him, we may have been told in subtle or not so subtle ways that we are too much and our ideas are too far out there. We may have been discouraged from taking actions to break through the status quo and be innovative in our work. We may have tamed our authentic selves to conform or to not cause any trouble.

The security guards in the video could be a metaphor for the critics you deal with as you collaborate with others to remove barriers to student success. They may be a metaphor for the negative self-talk that runs in your mind as you consider launching a tutoring or coaching business to share your expertise and help others reach their potential. Either way, it's essential that we not only think about what role these security guards play in our lives but how we might prevent them from blocking us from living our purpose to the fullest. According to Dr. Brené Brown, "Owning our story can be hard, but not nearly as difficult as spending our lives running from it. Embracing our vulnerabilities is risky, but not nearly as dangerous as giving up on love and belonging and joy—the experiences that make us the most vulnerable. Only when we are brave enough to explore the darkness will we discover the infinite power of our light."[7]

Jiggly Boy returned to a place where he was accepted and nurtured. He was surrounded by those who accepted him for who he was, and they experienced joy because of his presence. He had a support system. His family was with him and cheered him on with all his imperfections and vulnerabilities. When he was vulnerable and rose to the occasion, he was recognized by everyone in attendance, including the players, and rewarded with raucous applause. Finally, the person he was there to celebrate, Kevin Garnett, compassionately acknowledged what he did. His smile and gesture were proof that he appreciated Jiggly Boy. When we fully accept others and create conditions that include boundaries, trust, and nonjudgment, our students, colleagues, and those we serve can freely be themselves. The more we are free to be ourselves, the more successful we are, and success is measured by more than grades, test scores, and rankings on formal evaluations. Success is about our ability to operate in our purpose.

Sarah L. Johnson

Leadership Coach, Educator, Author, and Podcaster
Sarah Johnson Consulting
Wisconsin

Sarah is an exceptional educator and author who shares her journey through her blog, podcast, and social media, where she chronicles her running journey. Sarah Johnson's many layers become clear to me over time. She has faced and overcome several obstacles.

When I started out as an educator in the sunrise of my early twenties, my passion and energy could not be contained; my focus on students and helping to build curriculum and programs in our tiny school consumed my entire life. Over time, the pace shifted slightly because I had children of my own vying for that first position in my heart. When I took on my first principal role, I allowed my passion for leading a school to become all consuming, and it cost me contentment in my personal life. As I have learned to build better boundaries in all areas of my full life, I've shifted my focus from serving the students, staff, and community in just one building to aiding the adults who serve those groups across the country and world.

I've learned hard lessons in my own journey and created work aligned to my purpose of serving professionals. I want to help them avoid the mistakes I made or to recover after their own struggles. Only in recent years have I established my own mission, vision, and values to affirm my purpose in the work I do. Now my work is more centered on utilizing my passions and skills to impact others in all areas of life. That means empowering others to take hold of their own full lives so they live with purpose, passion, and priority. I can do this with great enthusiasm, knowing that the culmination of my experiences allows me to lead in this space with empathy, clarity, and service.

Over the course of my career, I have reached breaking points when I lost myself and needed an anchor to keep me from slipping away. As a teacher, it was easier to stay focused because the students were right in front of me. As a principal, I sometimes felt I needed divine intervention to keep me focused amid the stress. Now, as a consultant, coach, professor, speaker, and podcaster, my purpose is centered on the internal work I've done to create clarity about who I am, regardless of what role I serve in a given moment. I've had to let go of my traditional thinking about titles and reconcile my worth because leadership looks different from the model I had formed in my mind. I've had to quiet the noise of what others want from me, or what I perceive they want, and get clear on my mission and the vision of who I must become.

To do this, I've had to overcome impostor syndrome. My internal critic wanted to shut down my plans for amplifying others, publishing my thoughts on leadership, and coaching other leaders. And I had to fight my own default pattern of dreaming big and then dropping the details. When I chose to develop my own mission, vision, values, and goals, it was a game changer. I can now speak life into myself, and this allows me to do the same for others.

If there is an educator out there who can say they have never faltered in their passion for serving or felt disillusioned along their journey, I'd be blown over. I'd also think they weren't being honest with themselves. Each of us goes through stages in our career where we question whether we can still tackle the challenges we find ourselves facing. We know our profession has been bleeding for quite a while—attrition rates have increased by 50 percent since the nineties, according to one study[8]—so it's no surprise when an educator considers leaving. What is inspiring is when they choose to stay through those times of questioning.

The Path to Authenticity

Because this book is meant to help you learn how to improve school culture from the inside out, it's important that I describe ways you can become more authentic

One of the first things you must do on your journey to authenticity is become self-aware. In chapter 3, I described why establishing positive relationships is a key Be GREAT principle. Establishing positive relationships requires self-awareness, which is closely tied to being authentic. Self-awareness is a major mechanism influencing personal development.

I admire people who have a deep sense of self and can speak up about their needs, expectations, and boundaries in a respectful manner. Our polarized society has made it difficult for us to not shrink in the face of opposition or puff up to protect ourselves from criticism.[9] Neither one of these responses provides a pathway to authenticity.

A couple of years ago, I had an impromptu morning meeting at work. Around 7:50 a.m., I received a call from our receptionist letting me know a young man needed to see me. I asked her to send him to my office. When he entered, we greeted each other in our standard affirming manner, and then he sat down. His pretense for the meeting was a logistic request, but I could discern from his body language that he had a hidden purpose. He sat slumped in his chair, and through his mask, he asked, "How's your mental health?"

I was shocked by his question but took the bait. He wanted to talk about how he was feeling; his self-awareness had led him to ask for help. I responded by sharing a little bit about my weekend and how I felt. Then I pivoted and asked, "How are you doing? What's going on?"

He slumped further and shook his head, rubbing his forehead with his right hand. He said, "Man, Mr. Carter. I'm struggling . . ." I turned my chair to make sure I was directly facing him and leaned in to let him know that he had my undivided attention.

He opened up about his life, the real obstacles he was trying to overcome, and how overwhelmed he felt. The more he talked, the straighter he sat up in his chair and the more animated he became. According to consultant, writer, and expert on well-being technology Dr. Tchiki Davis, "Increasing self-awareness of false attitudes or inappropriate behaviors requires peace of mind, time, attention, and focus. Knowing ahead of time that we can indeed change in positive ways through deeper self-awareness makes it worth working on those personal qualities we most value. But first, we must look within ourselves through self-examination to see what's there, which is often less obvious than we think."[10]

I admired my student's self-awareness and willingness to talk about his struggles. He spoke about his future goals, and I assured him that we would do whatever it took to help him get there. We shared a few stories, and I gave him the information he came for. After about twenty minutes, he went to class ready to tackle the day. We were both fulfilled. I took away three reminders from our impromptu meeting:

- **Be accessible.** Accessibility is about displaying the kind of attitude that makes you approachable in the first place. Availability is about putting aside the to-do list and making time for others. I had a few things I felt I needed to get done before the first-period bell rang, but it was more important to meet with my student than to tackle my to-do list. The more accessible we are to others, the more likely they will be to express their true intentions, hopes, fears, and obstacles. Thus, they become more self-aware.

- **Be available.** I was open to listening to my student's story and available to provide emotional support and tangible help. I also let him know I was available to help anytime.

- **Be accountable.** Earlier in the school year, I noticed this young man seemed to be carrying a heavy burden, so I stopped him in the hall one day to check on him. He wasn't in the mood to talk much but assured me he was OK. I let him know that I'd be checking on him from time to time and that he could stop by the office anytime he needed to talk. Ultimately, he did just that.

Active Listening and Observation

Our minds are cluttered with so much information from texts, social media posts, emails, news reports, and flurries of digital images that it has become challenging to be an active listener. In chapter 3, I shared how being an active listener creates deeper connections with others. It is also an important factor in developing self-awareness. By taking your attention away from yourself and focusing on others, you can break any negative thought chain or self-talk loop that leads to sabotage. According to Dr. Tchiki Davis, "By being open to someone else, we can learn to listen objectively, even lovingly, to what that person wants or needs to share. This, in turn, helps teach us how to listen to our own inner dialogues and opinions objectively and lovingly as well."[11]

Active listening is a skill, or muscle, that gets stronger with practice. It may feel good to provide advice and solutions, but you may trample over someone who simply needs a sounding board. At the same time, you must learn to listen to your own thoughts and question the root of those thoughts. Notice patterns that emerge and when they emerge. Notice what you think about when you observe others and what it is that you observe. This data provides a lot of information about our core beliefs, values, and characteristics, and it can help you align them so you become your authentic self.

Self-Reflection

Self-reflection is one of the most important parts of your path to authenticity because it is a discipline that leads to growth and understanding of self. Dr. Geil Browning, the founder and CEO of Emergenetics International, stated, "Reflection is a deeper form of learning that allows us to retain every aspect of any experience, be it personal or professional—why something took place, what the impact was, whether it should happen again—as opposed to just remembering that it happened. It's about tapping into every aspect of the experience, clarifying our thinking, and homing in on what really matters to us."[12]

Through self-reflection, you can evaluate your interactions with others and how you feel during and after those interactions. This can help you understand what boundaries you need to establish, or reestablish, to find balance in life. For example, many educators may find it difficult to establish time boundaries because they are keen to help others, meet self-imposed deadlines, participate in professional development, connect with a personal learning network, stay on top of work-related tasks, and raise a family. During the pandemic, the time boundary was pretty much destroyed for the many people who worked from home because it became even more difficult to determine when to put away work and be present. Perhaps you realized you were giving too much time and attention to things beyond your control. Maybe you learned to be more present, you redefined what was important to you, and you became more balanced in your approach to work and life. It's becoming the norm for educators to take care of their mental health and wellness. Let's take advantage of this paradigm shift.

In my district, we often create moments for self-reflection at the end of a student project, after we introduce a new initiative to staff, or after leading a professional learning opportunity. It's something we intentionally plan for to ensure that learning is meaningful and has the potential to stick. Do you intentionally make time to self-reflect?

Identify Your Strengths

Have you ever questioned why you do what you do? Have you examined your passion for what you do? You can be passionate about something apart from your career and live a successful, fulfilled life.

Instead of questioning your passion, I encourage you to examine whether you are using your strengths as a path to living a more authentic life. If you feel like you're operating on autopilot or that you're stifled by your title or job description, you may be detached from your authentic self.

Several years ago, I began speaking and coaching while still serving as a building principal. I loved the work. I connected with peers who I am blessed to call my friends. I enjoyed helping other leaders and educators work through challenges and inspiring them to try new things. After a presentation or coaching session, I'd return to my building fired up and ready to take on the day. Others would notice my positive attitude. Soon after, however, I would become bogged down with the minutia of my job. Over time, I became discouraged and somewhat disheartened. I loved my staff, students, and community, which made it more difficult because I felt like I was not giving them my best. It was a struggle. I was approached about a principal position in another district, and after a lengthy interview process, I decided to change districts, hoping that I would find my joy in a fresh start.

I quickly learned that my issue wasn't the district or the position. My issue was internal. I still got a charge from being a building principal, especially from the relationships I established with staff members, students, and parents. I have fond memories of us working together to bring about positive changes, overcome challenges, and grow personally and professionally. But there were aspects of being a principal that I just couldn't stomach anymore.

In *The One Thing: The Surprisingly Simple Truth behind Extraordinary Results*, Gary Keller wrote, "Discover your purpose by asking yourself what drives you. What's the thing that gets you up in the morning and keeps you going when you're tired and worn down? I sometimes refer to this as your 'Big Why.' It's why you're excited with your life. It's why you're doing what you're doing. Absent an answer, pick a direction . . . Think of the ONE thing you want your life to be about more than any other . . . Pick a direction, start marching down that path, and see how you like it. Time brings clarity, and if you find you don't like it, you can always change your mind. It's your life."[13]

I thought about this quote a lot. After many months of reflection, talk therapy, and soul searching, I learned that the thing I enjoy most is teaching. Teaching isn't restricted to the classroom. It can take many forms, such as coaching, using staff meetings as learning opportunities, speaking, and presenting. I love the entire learning process, but because I had let myself get bogged down by the complexities of my principalship, I wasn't seeing as many daily teaching opportunities. They were definitely there, but I was just ready for something different. After several conversations with my wife and some mentors, I decided to leave the principalship to coach, present, and consult full-time. For the first time in a long time, I felt free.

In chapter 1, I introduced you to Jack Slavinski, the leadership coach I hired to help me and my building leadership team become more cohesive and stronger. Through that process and research-based strategies, I learned about my signature strengths. As a full-time coach, speaker, and presenter, I was able to more frequently use my strengths, and my mind was restored. My intention was to work primarily in Central Ohio, where I live, and travel no more than a few hours from home. However, I began receiving requests to coach in other parts of the country, such as California, Connecticut, and Kansas. I enjoyed the work, but I recognized that my time away from home—even though I was home more often than before—was taking a toll on my daughter. I had to ask myself, "If my one thing is teaching, what lessons am I teaching Gabby when I'm away from home for extended periods of time?"

After a year as a full-time leadership coach, consultant, and speaker, I applied for the principal position at Eastland Career Center. Despite my previous relationship with the district, leadership experience, and accolades, I didn't get the position. To be honest, it crushed my ego! I was embarrassed and felt shame rearing its ugly head. I had to quickly regroup and reflect on my purpose and priorities. I was offered the assistant principal role and humbly accepted it because I remembered how much I had enjoyed being an assistant principal before. My transition was not easy for the first month or two, but I learned to lean into my signature strengths and find ways to use them to impact my team, staff, and students positively. I had a better work-life wholeness, my mind was clearer, and I supported the principal and other district leaders with my many years of experience as a head principal and coach.

I soon discovered that I was able to be more authentic because I focused my efforts and energy on *leading up* instead of being *the* leader. It was rejuvenating! It reminded me of Shawn Achor's book *The Orange Frog: A Parable Based on Positive Psychology*, which is a story about how a positive attitude is contagious and helps create more happiness by helping others to contribute to the good of the culture.[14] The more I was able to help others, the more orange, or happy, I became.

Working with Jack Slavinski, I used the VIA Character Strengths Survey, a free research-based assessment,[15] to learn more about my signature strengths, which helped me understand how to live more authentically regardless of my role. My top five character strengths are as follows:

- **Love of learning:** I master new skills, topics, and bodies of knowledge, whether on my own or formally. This relates to my strength of curiosity but goes beyond it to describe my tendency to add systematically to what I know.

- **Perspective:** I'm able to provide wise counsel to others. I have ways of looking at the world that make sense to myself and others.

- **Humility:** I let my accomplishments speak for themselves. I don't regard myself as more special than I am.

- **Spirituality:** I have coherent beliefs about the higher purpose and meaning of life that shape my conduct and provide comfort. I know where I fit within the larger scheme.

- **Forgiveness:** I forgive those who have done wrong, accept others' shortcomings, and give people a second chance. I am not vengeful.

I have taken this assessment twice in the last few years, and my top five signature strengths have remained pretty consistent. Describing my strengths has allowed me to be more intentional about my daily work, establish even more meaningful relationships with others, understand my weaknesses, and identify my triggers. Learning my strengths is liberating because these are principles that come naturally—thus I am more authentic. Besides, according to Dr. Brené Brown, "When we don't give ourselves permission to be free, we rarely tolerate that freedom in others."[16]

In my current field, career technical education (CTE), I use my strengths to help my district. It wasn't about my position as assistant principal—it's about my disposition. I collaborated with district staff to plan our professional development and find ways to help our leaders by offering perspective, learning about the nuances of CTE, and connecting with students and staff. Bringing my authentic self to my district opened up an opportunity for a new position that allows me to serve a much broader audience in areas that align with my strengths and our goals as a district. I am now a member of the executive cabinet, serving as the director of student support systems. In this role,

I am responsible for identifying and removing barriers to student success. I oversee special education; multi-tiered systems of support; English-language learners; positive behavior interventions and supports; diversity, equity, and inclusion; social-emotional learning; and all things climate and culture.

If you are frustrated, disenchanted, discouraged, and questioning your effectiveness as a leader, teacher, coach, or anything else, take some time to identify your areas of strength. Reflect on the moments you experience joy in your work and consider why. Then do something about it. Take the VIA Character Strengths Survey and examine your profile to find ways to increase purpose in your career. Once you get your results, share your strengths with others and let them know how you will use them to serve your school. Accountability to others will provide the support you need on your path to authenticity. Your colleagues will experience the difference authenticity makes and thank you for it.

In chapter 3, I highlighted educator Stephanie Rothstein from the Santa Clara Unified School District. Stephanie asks her students to complete the True Colors personality assessment to get a better understanding of who they are, how they can connect with each other, and how she can foster deeper conversations in class. An added benefit is that her students learn more about themselves and are empowered to develop deeper self-awareness, confidence, and assurance. The VIA Character Strengths Survey and the True Colors personality assessment are based on research, not just emotion or perception. Combined, they provide not just students but educators a great starting point for pursuing authenticity by unpacking default behavior and relearning strategies to live a more fulfilled life. Once you are living authentically, you can help others do the same. Ralph Waldo Emerson was right when he said, "To be yourself in a world that is constantly trying to make you something else is the greatest accomplishment."

Be GREAT Tips on How to Be Authentic

I knew I wanted to be a teacher when I was in middle school, and that idea was solidified during my freshman year in college. I remember talking about the future with a good friend of mine. I said, "I'll be happy when I graduate from college." After I graduated, I said, "I'll be happy when I get a job." After I got a job, I said, "I'll be happy when I get a car, get braces, and get a house." It was always something else that would make me happy. These notions were based on others' ideas. I was not happy. And I had such a narrow view of what it meant to be a teacher that I was not being my authentic self. I became what I thought a teacher ought to be: the ultimate professional and nothing else.

I would advise you to love everything about yourself and stop just wishing for happiness. Look at happiness not as a destination but as a state of being. My happiness comes from simply being my authentic self. I must know who that person is, however. You must know who you are, too.

Spend time on self-discovery. Think about your likes, dislikes, wants, needs, hopes, triggers, aspirations, and inspirations. Take notice of what you think about and how you respond to certain situations. Don't waste your experiences as you wait to accomplish your next goal. To be more authentic, try the following actions:

- Pray or meditate more often.
- Develop self-awareness through journaling.
- See a therapist (if feasible) to help with self-understanding and to develop emotional intelligence.
- Heal your inner child.
- Listen to your body and understand your emotions.
- Focus less on being liked and more on being respected.
- Be comfortable with being uncomfortable.
- Use your voice.

Three Questions for Conversation

1 In what ways are you living—or not living—your core values?

2 How are you creating the conditions for others, especially your students, to be their authentic selves?

3 What would you need to change to live a more authentic life personally and professionally?

SIX

BE TEACHABLE

*I live my life in a state of
continuous improvement.*

—Dr. Kim Pietsch Miller

We have twenty-four seven access to any bit of information we want, from video content to professional journals. We are, by choice and by design, inundated with content, so learning is no longer relegated to the schoolhouse. When we have questions, we ask Siri, or we use Google. When we want to learn about a new restaurant, we go to Yelp. When we contemplate making another purchase from Amazon, we read the comments about that product to learn about others' experiences. If we want to learn how to do a home repair, we can talk to friends, but it's more likely we'll search YouTube. Video has become a vital medium for learning. According to researcher Dave Davies, "YouTube receives more than 2 billion logged-in users per month and feeds over 1 billion hours of video each day to users (that's right ... billion)."[1] We willingly gather data to make an informed decision because the information is readily available. It's part of the learning process and a valuable attribute of what it means to be teachable.

When I began teaching in 1994, email was relatively new, information was not as readily accessible, and professional development was something I expected should come from my district—and it did. I worked with some outstanding building and district administrators who planned evidence-based and relevant professional learning opportunities for the staff. I can't say with certainty that I took advantage of every opportunity offered, but I got my fair share. What I definitely took advantage of were the informal lunchtime and planning-period conversations with my colleagues and administrators. I loved listening to their stories. I gleaned strategies from them for how to become a better educator. My mantra was that I wanted my students to be thinkers. To think, one must be a learner, and I tried to model that. In chapter 4, I described the time my mother corrected my behavior by reminding me that nothing was going to be given to me. I had to perform consistently to earn it. That lesson continues to be a driving force behind my desire to learn.

By the time I was tapped to be trained as a Critical Friends Group facilitator in 1998, I had shifted my thinking. I had started to take ownership of my professional growth. I realized it was no one else's responsibility. While I enjoyed district professional learning days, they were inadequate because there were simply not enough days in the school calendar to satisfy my need for effective professional learning. According to the Coalition of Essential Schools, "A Critical Friends Group (CFG) brings together four to ten teachers within a school over at least two years, to help each other look seriously at their own classroom practice and make changes in it. After a solid grounding in group process skills, members focus on designing learning goals for students which can be stated specifically enough that others can observe them in operation."[2]

I recognized that not all teachers I worked with were given the same opportunities as me, so I did not take this position for granted. It was humbling, and I doubted I was even qualified for such an important role. As a trained facilitator, I was asked to hold meetings, lead sessions during an in-service day, and participate in teacher leadership and instruction committees. As my exposure and experience accumulated, my teachable spirit came alive.

To be teachable means to have a willingness to learn by being taught. The operative word is *willingness*. The following are several key definitions of willingness:

- Cheerful compliance (according to WordNet, a Princeton University database)[3]
- The quality of being happy to do something if it is needed (according to *Cambridge Dictionary*)[4]
- Not opposed to, in mind (according to Definitions.net)[5]

All three definitions point to one's attitude and actions. You cannot be forced to learn something new, to change your mind, or to change your behavior. However, you can be influenced to do so if you have a teachable spirit. I'm grateful for the influence of some exceptional educators and mentors who asked me thought-provoking questions, exposed me to opportunities for continuous improvement, and provided constructive criticism, acknowledgment, and praise. But I had to be willing to accept what they offered. It was this mindset that helped me to establish a personal learning network (PLN).

Be Teachable and Teach Others

Oliver Wendell Holmes Jr. once said, "The mind, once stretched by a new idea, never returns to its original dimensions."[6] Five years into my principalship, I became a connected educator. I expanded my PLN to include others outside my district. My mind was stretched by seeing how others were leading and by imagining the possibilities of what our profession could become. I participated in and facilitated professional chats and book studies on social media, listened to webinars, and asked more reflective questions. I started blogging to share stories of the amazing work my staff and students were doing and to share my reflections on leadership, education, and school culture. I shared what I learned with my staff in a variety of ways.

Access to and opportunities for professional development have increased greatly due to technology, the need for more relevant and timely learning, and a growing dissatisfaction with the traditional model of "sit and get." Don't misunderstand me; I thoroughly enjoy attending quality professional conferences as a presenter and participant. I enjoy listening to and learning from dynamic speakers, attending a variety of breakout sessions, and connecting with other educators to discuss hot topics and share best practices. But there are options besides attending professional conferences.

We can engage in meaningful and relevant learning experiences on our own time, at our own pace, and in the place of our choosing. We must accept that learning is a twenty-four seven endeavor every day of the year. It is not bound to traditional office hours. Technology has equalized the traditional professional development model by providing many opportunities for those who want to take responsibility for their own growth and development. While technology can distract from connection sometimes (people fixate on their screens instead of each other), it can, when consciously employed for this purpose, also promote connections by compensating for long distances and different time zones. The following are seven effective professional development resources for educators:

- **Webinars:** Webinars are web-based presentations where participants interact with each other and a presenter. Due to the global pandemic, there is no shortage of webinars. They are often free and typically occur after the school day.

- **Podcasts:** Podcasts are web-based conversations about a particular topic. Most podcasts are recorded live and archived for future use. Like webinars, podcasts are popular, and the topics discussed are as diverse as they come. The challenge is to search through what's out there to find ones that are meaningful to you.

- **Twitter chats and Spaces:** A Twitter chat is a topic-based discussion on Twitter that is curated using a specific hashtag. Thousands of educators participate in weekly chats, and school districts host their own chats to continue conversations beyond the school day. Twitter Spaces are private chat rooms centered on specific topics. Participants engage in conversations for a designated period of time.

- **Blogs:** Blogs make learning visible because blogging is a reflective process that showcases thoughts, ideas, successes, and struggles. There are many free blog sites, such as Edublogs, Blogger, and WordPress, that educators use for their own professional and personal growth. Through my own blog, I've found a global community.

- **YouTube:** YouTube is the third-largest search engine in the world! If there's a topic you want to learn more about, I'm certain you'll find plenty of videos about it if you search on YouTube. Even better, you could create your own YouTube channel to share your expertise with others.

- **Zoom/Microsoft Teams/Google Meet:** Videoconferencing became a staple during the pandemic. It removes time and distance barriers and provides a means to engage in conversation with groups or individuals to discuss relevant topics. Additionally, it provides digital face-to-face interaction, which is important for maintaining connection.

- **Facebook Groups:** Facebook Groups are a popular way to connect with others who share your interests. They facilitate organic discussion, learning, and awareness about specific topics. Whatever your interest, there is likely a Facebook Group dedicated to it.

Be Curious

When I became a principal, I strived to enhance the professional learning culture that I had experienced as a teacher and assistant principal. In those previous roles, I was encouraged to focus on continuous improvement, take ownership of my learning, and be willing to learn. As I learned from educators outside my district and benefited from the relationships I established with them, I grew. As a principal, I wanted to encourage my staff and colleagues to do the same. Insatiable curiosity is at the core of being teachable, and a key attribute of being a learner is a desire to teach. Under the leadership of Gregg Morris and Mark White, I learned to empower teachers in new ways. I gleaned three strategies to support staff learning and decided to implement them.

When I observed an innovative idea or outstanding teaching and learning, I invited the teachers to share their experiences with others at a local, state, or national conference. I encouraged them to submit a proposal because I was proud of their work and wanted to reward them with a trip to a conference where they could share their expertise and connect with like-minded professionals.

I also worked with our dean of curriculum, assistant principals, and department chairs to identify those who were modeling best and next practices and create space for them to share at staff meetings. What better way to build capacity around instructional practices than to create the conditions for staff to hear from their peers? It's important to use a process that allows for reflection, feedback, and discussions about next steps.

Sometimes it's good for teachers to hear from another expert in the field—someone who has successfully modeled or thoroughly researched different ways to accomplish a task. I learned that inviting relevant speakers to your school can help ignite or support professional learning. Making this investment shows your level of commitment to your staff, and it reinforces expectations.

In addition to the strategies above, remember to encourage others to be curious through reflection, collaboration, and relevant professional learning.

Reflect

Sometimes our minds get cluttered by the content we consume: tweets, text messages, podcasts, books, conversations, talk radio, and Instagram and Facebook posts. According to retired school social worker and parent educator Libby Simon, "Information overload is infecting our lives and is multiplied exponentially when we are forced to wade through dizzying amounts of information to make simple everyday decisions."[7] Consuming this much information can impact your ability to ponder, wonder, or reflect, and you might unknowingly drift on autopilot. This is comfortable and easy, but it is counterproductive. If you stop being curious and stop reflecting, you stop being teachable. You must create boundaries when it comes to accessing content.

Several years ago, I had to attend the funeral of my wife's two-month-old great-nephew. The funeral was in Georgia, which is about a ten-hour trip from Ohio by car, so I had a lot of time to think. As I observed two young parents mourning the sudden and tragic passing of their son, I thought about how much we take life for granted.

The global pandemic has made us all reflect on this. We've been forced to slow down, open our eyes, listen more carefully to others, and examine ourselves. We get caught up in what we don't have or who has more. We focus on the things that divide us as opposed to what draws us closer together. We run on autopilot until we are interrupted by a tragedy. Curiosity and reflection can jump-start our learning and switch off our autopilot. We can start by asking ourselves several *what if* questions:

PERSONAL/FAMILY

- What if we took five minutes to pray or meditate every day?
- What if families had breakfast or dinner together at least twice a week?
- What if we exercised for thirty minutes every day?
- What if we watched less TV and read, wrote, and talked with others more?
- What if we spent less money and gave more?
- What if we gave three hugs a day?
- What if we genuinely complimented at least five people a day?
- What if we chose to learn from failure?
- What if we forgave more often and extended the grace we, too, desire?
- What if we chose one day a week to turn off our mobile devices, desktops, and TVs?
- What if we created a bucket list and actually did it?
- What if we weren't afraid?

SCHOOL

- What if every staff member believed all students could learn at high levels?
- What if schools truly focused on learning for all?
- What if every student felt like they belonged?
- What if every parent felt like they had a partnership with their child's teachers?
- What if principals truly made classroom visits and visibility a daily priority?
- What if principals weren't afraid to confront behaviors that run counter to the school vision, mission, and values?
- What if, for one night a week, there was no homework assigned?
- What if the senior year was more relevant?
- What if teachers were inspired to work in our schools?
- What if students were passionate about learning in our classes?

- What if students were given the chance to recover from an academic failure?

I can't help but think about the words spoken by the two-month-old's mother as she courageously addressed the guests at the funeral: "Even though he wasn't with us long, he brought so much peace to this family and brought us all together. I hurt, but I can't help but to be happy for what he has done for this family."

Her words caused me to reflect upon the many questions listed above. Allow yourself to ponder them, too. What are we going to do with the time we have? What if we picked just two questions from each list and took the time to apply them to our lives? Imagine what a significant impact you would have on others.

As you reflect on your current situation, start thinking about how you will support learning for all students as well as yourself. Consider trying one of the strategies mentioned above and be sure to explain to your staff what you hope to accomplish.

Be Teachable = Take a Risk

I can't swim, but ten years ago I ventured to upstate New York to conquer the Indian and Hudson Rivers via whitewater rafting. It was an amazing experience. The weather was simply horrible, but it added to the mystique of the adventure. I was invited to participate in a guys-only weekend trip by my friend Steve Bollar. It was an annual trip for him and a group of his friends, but this was the first time I joined them.

Our adventure began on a Friday with a five-and-a-half-hour drive from Philadelphia to North Creek, New York. The only guy I knew was Steve, so the road trip was one of the most important parts of our journey. We talked, laughed, reflected on life, and developed friendships along the way. Without this time, the overall experience would not have been as great as it was. Nearly every meaningful experience in life boils down to the relationships you have with others.

Once we hit the water on Saturday, we spent several hours rafting during the seventeen-mile trek along the Hudson River. The backdrop was the Adirondack Mountains, a sixty-degree temperature, and rain. Did I mention I can't swim?

As I reflect on our trip, I realize I learned a great deal about being teachable. To do something new, someone must initiate change. Steve Bollar was the connector of this trip. He'd done this before and invited friends from New Jersey, Maryland, Pennsylvania, and Ohio. Without Steve taking the initiative to set this up, the trip would not have occurred. Leaders take charge, research, and create new opportunities for others to grow. They are open to new experiences regardless of prior knowledge or comfort.

As a leader, influence matters. When Steve first asked me to attend, I thought of every excuse not to: I couldn't swim, I had an administrative luncheon, and I needed to be at school (even though the students were gone). Steve listened to my excuses, but then he followed up by sharing his past experiences of whitewater rafting. He also talked passionately about the friends he wanted me to meet. By the time he was finished, I couldn't say no! Leaders don't just present facts; they also tell compelling stories to convey a particular message. I wanted to experience what he experienced, and I envisioned what I could learn about myself and others during the trip.

To be teachable, we must be willing to communicate with people we don't know that well. Since three of the six guys in the raft had never been whitewater rafting, communication was key. However, the aspect of communication I'm referring to is listening. We had to listen very closely to our guide, who was not only highly qualified but very effective. When learning something, we must identify and listen to the experts.

It's much easier to go through rough waters with others. Tough times are inevitable, but going through them alone is not. *We* is much better than *me*.

Take a chance and learn something new. How can we as educators and leaders expect others to try new things if we don't? Model what you expect, and you'll see more of it. I mention this because, as I stated earlier, I can't swim, so to go whitewater rafting was a major stretch for me. At one point during the trip, we came upon an extremely large boulder sticking out of the water. Our guide indicated that we could climb the boulder and jump off into the twenty-foot-deep river. I thought, "Yeah, right. I'm going to sit right here." As we got closer to the rock, we all started looking at each other, and one by one, I heard the others say, "I'm in!" I had this internal conflict going on and thought, "If you jump and die, your wife is going to kill you!" Then I thought, "But I'm with a number of people that can swim, I've got on the right equipment, and others have shown it's safe, so what's the worst that could happen?" After much contemplation, I finally said, "I'm in!" I climbed the rock with the help of our guide, approached the edge, looked down, backed up, took three big steps, held my nose, and . . . splash! I can still feel the warm, clean, fresh water taking me in. Everything just stopped.

That was an aha moment for me. Why? I realized that if we as leaders provide the right training, modeling, resources, support, and environment for others to take risks, the possibilities of what we can accomplish together are endless.

Steve Bollar

Leadership Coach, Speaker, and Consultant
Stand Tall Enterprises
Burlington, New Jersey

Steve Bollar is one of the most dynamic educational leaders I know. His wit, intelligence, positive attitude, and teachable spirit have helped him to impact the lives of others as a leadership coach, speaker, and consultant. He has over twenty years of experience as an educator and has been an elementary school art teacher, middle school principal, assistant superintendent, and superintendent. He captures the hearts and minds of thousands of educators and students through engaging storytelling and sharing ideas about school culture. He shares how being teachable has contributed to his success.

Our education careers evolve. We get out of college or whatever formal training and are ready to go and teach others what we know. But we quickly realize something when we get into our formal teaching positions: we have more learning to do. This was true with me. I was an art teacher. Being an art teacher, I knew I had a talent that others didn't have. I'd mastered a specific subject. Others enjoyed art but felt unsure about their artistic abilities. Obviously, I knew it all. The young, arrogant, and ignorant me learned quickly that it isn't all about one specific talent. Realizing that I didn't know enough and needed to learn more made me better at everything. And this process is ongoing. Specifically, I continue to learn from the mistakes I make.

The art and practice of continual reflection is a powerful teaching tool. Pausing to think about what was done and how it was done allows time for growth. Once that reflection takes place, however, many forget about the next step. That next step is to seek resources and advice from others to ensure that we make the necessary adjustments to continue to become better. Don't just stay in your own head. Become teachable. Don't just learn what to do; learn what not to do. Success!

Being teachable isn't always easy. As educators, we have a ton on our plate. There are so many reports, standards, meetings, and levels of accountability that it's almost impossible to actually teach. It's tempting to get into a routine that allows you to operate on autopilot versus make an impact. This is what I consider the difference between compliance and commitment.

Being compliant is a lower level of accomplishment. Yes, you will get results and some quality outcomes. It's a comfortable spot to be in. It is doing what is expected of you and checking off the boxes. Being committed is a higher level of accomplishment. When you are committed, you are intentional about your growth and the need to be better. Educating and leading others is not just a job that you must do each day. You accept that comfort is a luxury. Being uncomfortable because you are struggling and learning and being teachable is what will make you and those that look to you better. Compliance will take care of itself when you are committed to your goals, mission, and values. That includes being teachable.

Being teachable isn't always about learning the best strategy, developing a quality relationship, or being positively influenced by someone. Sometimes it's about learning what strategy not to use and staying true to your own beliefs and values.

As a new assistant principal, I was excited and ready to learn how to be a powerful educational leader. The principal was an established leader in the school and community. I knew I would grow and learn so much from her. As the school year went on, I started to notice some things. The principal led from the office. Teachers feared talking to her. Students were chastised when wrong. If you were loyal to the office, the office was loyal to you.

Parents were partners only when they followed the rules. As a new administrator, I started to think, "I guess this is what administration is like."

The turning point for me was when a grandfather brought his grandson back to the school after hours and insisted on going to the classroom to talk to the teacher about the day's lesson. I witnessed the principal stop them at the door and not let them pass. The grandfather was very upset and insisted he and his grandson must go back to the classroom and "get this lesson right!" He wasn't very well-spoken and continued attempting to explain. The principal dug her heels in and very directly stated why the man and his grandson would not be going back to the classroom. She had me and the other assistant principal escort them out of the school. I learned a valuable lesson that day. The lesson was not about how to prevent people from coming into the school—it was about how not to treat parents, grandparents, and the community.

While escorting the grandfather and grandson out of the building, I asked questions. It turned out the grandson had lied about the work he was supposed to do. The grandfather was teaching him an old-school lesson by making him go back to get the notes from the board and hopefully talk to the teacher to get clarity. He just wanted to help his grandson the best way he knew how.

I've told other educators that I learned more from that principal than anyone else in education. I learned the importance of being teachable and using my values as a filter for the lessons that I learn. Being teachable needs to sit well with your soul. Your own values should always be the filter through which you interpret your lessons.

Steve's message can be summarized by these words from John C. Maxwell: "Teachability is not so much about competence and mental capacity as it is about attitude. It is the desire to listen, learn, and apply. It is the hunger to discover and grow. It is the willingness to learn, unlearn, and relearn."[8]

Dr. Kimberly Pietsch Miller

Superintendent
Eastland-Fairfield Career & Technical Schools
Groveport, Ohio

Dr. Miller is an energetic and intelligent school leader with over thirty years of experience as a classroom teacher, middle school and high school administrator, district office staff member, superintendent, and presenter. I began this chapter with a message she has shared with our staff a couple of times: "I live my life in a state of continuous improvement." Her openness to learning, humility when taking risks, and willingness to ask good questions have been pathways to success.

I love to learn and grow, so I tend to look for opportunities to do so in new ways. I've pursued additional formal education throughout my career, from getting my master's degree and additional licenses to finally finishing my doctoral program in 2018. I have also been open to roles in new districts, cities, and educational settings. I've worked in urban, suburban, and rural districts. I've worked in elementary, middle, and high schools, as well as central offices. I've also held positions in traditional K–12 districts, an educational service center, higher education, and now in a career and technical school. I tend to thrive on being in new environments where I have a learning curve. I like asking questions and developing new knowledge and skills. I think that my willingness to learn (be teachable) has opened doors and brought me to this point in my journey.

Being a learner is just part of who I am. And I am intentional about it. I seek instruction from others. I will put myself in new and even uncomfortable situations so that I can learn something—even if I disagree with what I'm learning. If I can learn about another person's perspective, I believe that will benefit me as a leader. More importantly, it will benefit those I am leading.

The reality is that crises and difficult circumstances have caused me to pivot and learn. I don't know if I can point to just one situation. It would be easy to say the pandemic—that has caused all of us to pivot and learn. But whenever things go wrong or not as planned, leaders must pivot. And each time I have, I've learned a little more about how to be flexible, and I've realized that I have time to think, seek input from others, and make strategic decisions. Some situations require an immediate reaction, but most can be handled with patience. You can respond rather than react.

Educators may struggle with being teachable out of fear of being judged, rejected, or criticized. I teach a graduate course on leading change. In that course, I try to help students learn to analyze change efforts of other leaders so that they will be able to analyze their own actions, strengths, and challenges when they are leading. In one assignment, the students are asked to talk to educational leaders about a change effort they led that went well and one that did not. The challenge my students face is that many leaders don't want to admit their failures. If you can't admit when you've failed, you can't learn new ways of approaching a challenge or problem.

I try to create a culture of safety that allows those I lead to take on new learning and accept that short-term failure may result. If they can admit to the failure, they can learn from it. Failure is a part of learning. Just as a baby falls when they first begin to walk, we all stumble when learning. If leaders have not been coached on analyzing their actions for success or struggle, or if they can't admit the struggles, I think learning will be very difficult for them.

As educators, we should model being a learner and being teachable. I don't think we should expect anything of students that we don't expect of ourselves. If students are to take risks in their learning, then we should be doing the same. If we are not learners ourselves, we are not credible to students and risk holding them back. The world evolves. If our schools don't evolve, then we are not preparing students for a world beyond the schoolhouse, and that is just not acceptable. Our students count on us to provide the education they need for their futures, not our past. That requires learning.

One of the key components of any educational organization should be organized learning. That requires leaders to be the lead learners. Time must be intentionally invested in the learning of the leaders and all the adults in the organization. Too often we focus on the nuts and bolts of operations or the urgency of situations. But if we want learning leaders, we must invest in the learning of the people in our schools—and that starts with the educators.

Dr. Miller remains curious and takes calculated risks to adapt to changing times. She cultivates these same attributes in others because she sees it as her responsibility as a leader to prepare students for life beyond school. That's something we all strive to do, and it is our responsibility, regardless of position or title, to create the type of culture that enables every student to develop intellectually, socially, emotionally, and cognitively.

Be GREAT Tips on How to Be Teachable

While pursuing knowledge of your craft and subject matter, explore outside interests so that you become a more well-rounded person and broaden your perspective in ways that will create more learning opportunities for yourself and others. Fearing failure and seeing it as a flaw can be paralyzing. Being teachable develops resilience because it is about taking risks, pressing ahead, asking questions, and learning from mistakes. Show grace and mercy to your students and colleagues, but also show it to yourself. To be more teachable, remember these actions:

- Ask for help sooner to avoid self-made emergencies.
- Listen to understand instead of to respond.
- Judge less and empathize more.
- Express gratitude for lessons learned instead of moving on to the next thing.
- Ask clarifying questions even if you fear being seen as incompetent.
- Say yes more than no.

Three Questions for Conversation

1 How do you respond when you listen to, read the words of, or talk with others who differ from you?

2 What have you learned that's changed your life in the last year?

3 What is something you are looking forward to learning more about and why?

CONCLUSION

*God provides the wind, but
man must raise the sails.*

—St. Augustine

Some of the best experiences of my life have happened because I am an educator. I absolutely love what I do. I still have a hard time believing all that I have been able to accomplish. I do not take it for granted.

George Couros has a podcast called *The Innovator's Mindset*,[1] and it features a recurring episode theme centered on asking guests three questions:

- Which teacher inspired you?
- Which administrator inspired you?
- What advice would you give your first-year self?

I want to focus on the last question. When he asked me that question, I flashed back to my twenty-two-year-old self and thought about how uptight I was. I was regimented and followed routines. I worked until ten thirty or eleven each night grading papers, writing lesson plans, studying, and looking for engaging activities. I stressed about my students' performance and focused on my desire to teach them how to think critically. I rarely did anything outside of school because I coached three sports, was the Youth to Youth adviser, and attended many after-school activities. School was my life. Looking back at it, I wonder if I was even having fun.

The advice I would give my twenty-two-year-old self is to relax. Now, telling myself to relax rarely succeeds because that is not a strategy that works. How do I relax if I have programmed myself to keep going until I reach utter exhaustion?

I want to go a little deeper with that advice. I would not only tell myself to relax but teach myself how to cultivate a practice of *gratitude* and reinforce strategies to establish positive *relationships* with people outside of school, not just inside. I would tell myself to remember my purpose with *enthusiasm* and joy. I would spend more time becoming my *authentic* self instead of the person I thought others wanted to see. I would applaud myself for being *teachable* while being confident at the same time. I would tell myself that through my journey of developing and implementing the Be GREAT principles, my beliefs about students, staff, community, parents, curriculum, instruction, assessment, and leadership would become crystal clear. Here they are:

Students

- I believe all students can and will learn.
- I believe students are the reason why we are here and we have our jobs.
- I believe engaged students will exceed our expectations.

- I believe the more we know about our students, the better we will be at creating the conditions for them to grow.
- I believe in the development of the whole child: intellectually, emotionally, socially, physically, and spiritually.
- I believe student voice and student choice lead to more engaged and active learners and leaders.
- I believe successful schools promote the seven A's: academics, attendance, attitude, acts of service, athletics, arts, and activities. These create a sense of belonging for every student.

Staff

- I believe teachers are the most important factor in student success.
- I believe we are greater as a team than as individuals.
- I believe we are responsible for our own professional development and must continue to be learners.
- I believe in the power of a personal learning network for support, encouragement, learning, and sharing.
- I believe we are responsible for telling our positive story to recognize the behaviors and work we want to see more of. This leads to positive behavior and positive results.
- I believe we are highly skilled professionals who are passionate about our craft.
- I believe teacher leadership is a major element of the success of a school.

Community and Parents

- I believe we are partners with parents and the community in the development of students.
- I believe in engaging parents in the learning process in a variety of ways.

- I believe trusting relationships with parents and the community improve the overall performance of students.
- I believe when we care for our students, we gain the respect of parents and the community and therefore increase their support.

Curriculum, Instruction, and Assessment

- I believe common assessments improve instruction, make collaboration meaningful, and increase student achievement.
- I believe in a strong literacy program that includes reading and writing across the curriculum. I believe we should have a common writing rubric created by teachers that is used across the curriculum.
- I believe rigorous learning is a result of relevant lesson design and positive classroom relationships.
- I believe in students reading common texts to reinforce shared knowledge, and I believe in choice reading. This gives students a chance to examine common themes across a variety of texts, perspectives, and cultural identities.
- I believe students learn by doing, so an active and engaging learning environment is important.
- I believe learning is a messy, nonlinear process.
- I believe learning is our one constant. Time, resources, and location are variables.
- I believe in implementing formative instructional practices to personalize learning for all students.
- I believe we must teach critical thinking, creativity, collaboration, and communication through our content.
- I believe great teaching and learning create a great school.
- I believe there is more than one way to teach effectively.
- I believe in examining student work to evaluate the effectiveness of curriculum, instruction, and assessment.

- I believe healthy school environments reflect upon and respond to data to make decisions about curriculum, instruction, and assessment.
- I believe grades should be a reflection of what students know and are able to do.
- I believe in assessment retakes, which enable students to demonstrate mastery.
- I believe we must have some common beliefs about grading and assessment to provide equitable opportunities in our classrooms.

Leadership

- I believe a positive school culture promotes academic success, makes learning more relevant, and encourages positive behavior.
- I believe in establishing positive relationships among students, staff, and parents.
- I believe we learn through failure—as long as we fail forward. We should take calculated risks to stretch our students and ourselves.
- I believe in adaptive leadership, which means implementing a variety of strategies to problem solve, think critically, make decisions, and serve others, depending on the situation.
- I believe the principal is the most influential person in the school, for better or worse.
- I believe people lead change, not programs, and it's always about people.
- I believe a shared vision, shared values, and shared norms lead to a positive school climate.
- I believe in continuous improvement, which means we are in a constant state of learning, growth, and reflection.

- I believe there are three types of leadership decisions: mine, yours, and ours.
- I believe leaders ought to serve others.
- I believe trust is created by consistent interactions that create connection, demonstrate solid character, and result in competent actions.

As you embark on your journey to Be GREAT, think about your beliefs and reflect on the questions I shared in chapter 1:

- How do you want to be remembered?
- How can you best serve others throughout your day?
- When do you have a more positive attitude and experience the most joy throughout your day?
- What has led you to this point in your life?
- What can you do to be a better person?

Enjoy every step along the way, and #BeGREAT!

NOTES

CHAPTER 1

1   Thomas Oppong, "Psychologists Explain How Emotions, Not Logic, Drive Human Behaviour," Medium, accessed March 2, 2022, medium.com/personal-growth/psychologists-explain-how-emotions -not-logic-drive-human-behaviour-6ed0daf76e1a (the author deleted this story).

2   Sean Deveney, "Hall of Famer Maurice Cheeks Recalls National Anthem Assist: 'I Didn't Know I Would Do That,'" *Sporting News*, September 7, 2018, sportingnews.com/us/nba/news/maurice-m o-cheeks-national-anthem-natalie-gilbert-video-coach-nba-hall-of -fame-trail-blazers/h749s8eomo4l1gy86ju2g9r26.

3   Kim Elstun, "The Power of Words a Girl Changed a Blind Man Day Amazing," YouTube video, 2:00, January 7, 2014, youtube.com/ watch?v=QYcXTlGLUgE.

4   George Couros, "Helping Someone Get Better or Showing Them You Are Better?," *George Couros* (blog), March 15, 2018, georgecouros.ca/ blog/archives/8138.

5   Friedrich Nietzsche, "When We Are Tired, We Are Attacked by Ideas We Conquered Long Ago," QuoteInvestigator.com, February 26, 2019, quoteinvestigator.com/2019/02/26/tired/?msclkid =1133aadfc4bb11eca1aa7e4877ae2759.

CHAPTER 2

1   Ron J. West, *Corporate Caterpillars: How to Grow Wings* (iUniverse, 2013), 109.

2   Booker T. Washington, ed. Louis R. Harlen and Raymond W. Smock, asst. ed. Barbara S. Kraft, *The Booker T. Washington Papers Volume 5: 1899-1900* (Champaign, IL: University of Illinois Press, 1976), 501.

3   Todd Whitaker, *Shifting the Monkey: The Art of Protecting Good People from Liars, Criers, and Other Slackers* (Bloomington, IN: Solution Tree Press, 2014).

4   John C. Maxwell, *The 21 Indispensable Qualities of a Leader: Becoming the Person Others Will Want to Follow* (Nashville: Thomas Nelson, 2012).

5   Deepak Chopra, "The Use and Misuse of Gratitude," HuffPost, last updated May 22, 2012, huffpost.com/entry/gratitude_b_1364347.

6   SoulPancake, "An Experiment in Gratitude: The Science of Happiness," YouTube video, 7:13, July 11, 2013, youtube.com/watch?v=oHv6vTKD6lg.

7   Brené Brown, "Brené Brown on Joy and Gratitude," Global Leadership Network, November 21, 2018, globalleadership.org/articles/leading-yourself/brene-brown-on-joy-and-gratitude/.

8   Prakhar Verma, "Destroy Negativity from Your Mind with This Simple Exercise," Medium, November 27, 2017, medium.com/the-mission/a-practical-hack-to-combat-negative-thoughts-in-2-minutes-or-less-cc3d1bddb3af.

9   Rita Pierson, "Every Kid Needs a Champion," filmed April 2013 in New York, NY, TED video, 7:49, ed.ted.com/lessons/oM5nk8Rv.

10 "The 5 R's of Renaissance," Jostens Renaissance Education, September 29, 2016, jostensrenaissance.com/ohio-tour-16/.

11 Steve Bollar, "Stand Tall Leadership Show Episode 23 Ft. Kim Strobel," December 1, 2020, *Stand Tall Leadership Show*, podcast, website, 40:55, pod.co/stand-tall/stand-tall-leadership-show-episode-23-ft-kim-strobel.

12 Blokehead, *Five Minute Journal* (Createspace, 2014).

13 Jeff Thompson, "Resilience and the Practice of Gratitude," *Psychology Today* (blog), March 29, 2020, psychologytoday.com/us/blog/beyond-words/202003/resilience-and-the-practice-gratitude.

14 Amy Morin, "7 Scientifically Proven Benefits of Gratitude That Will Motivate You to Give Thanks Year-Round," *Forbes*, November 23,

2014, forbes.com/sites/amymorin/2014/11/23/7-scientifically
-proven-benefits-of-gratitude-that-will-motivate-you-to-give-thanks
-year-round/?sh=3ff69719183c.

15 "Gratitude Quiz," *Greater Good Magazine*, accessed April 20,
2022, greatergood.berkeley.edu/quizzes/take_quiz/gratitude.

CHAPTER 3

1 Shawn Achor, *Big Potential: How Transforming the Pursuit of Success
Raises Our Achievement, Happiness, and Well-Being* (New York:
Currency, 2018), 19.

2 Pamela Cantor, "The Power of Positive Relationships," *Summit
Learning Blog*, July 24, 2018, blog.summitlearning.org/2018/07/
positive-relationships/.

3 Paul J. Zak, "The Neuroscience of Trust," *Harvard Business Review*,
January–February 2017, hbr.org/2017/01/the-neuroscience-of-trust.

4 "Leadership Principles: How to Build Trust in the Virtual
Workspace," Focus 3, accessed on October 20, 2020, focus3.com/
leadership-principles-how-to-build-trust-in-the-virtual-workspace/.

5 Kelsey Ji, "Slowing Down Daily Life in a Virtual Age," *Daily
Princetonian*, February 14, 2021, dailyprincetonian.com/
article/2021/02/slow-daily-life-virtual-quarantine-dating-classes
-tiktok-technology-internet.

6 George Couros, "A Year of Yes! A Convo with Stephanie Rothstein:
The #InnovatorsMindset Podcast, Season 2 Ep 3," YouTube video,
49:03, January 17, 2021, youtube.com/watch?v=AcUJtkWD4qw.

7 Dwight L. Carter, Gary Sebach, and Mark White, *What's in Your
Space? 5 Steps for Better School and Classroom Design* (Thousand
Oaks, CA: Corwin, 2016), 8.

8 Jason Headley, "It's Not about the Nail," YouTube video, 1:41, May
22, 2013, youtube.com/watch?v=-4EDhdAHrOg.

9 KC Ifeanyi, "'Selma' Director Ava DuVernay Raises Her Hand for
Diversity in Hollywood in a Big Way," *Fast Company*, November
11, 2015, fastcompany.com/3053516/selma-director-ava-duverna
y-raises-her-hand-for-diversity-in-hollywood-in.

10   Saul McLeod, "Social Identity Theory," Simply Psychology, last
     updated October 24, 2019, simplypsychology.org/social-identity
     -theory.html.

11   Pabdoo, "Social Identity Wheel," Inclusive Teaching, accessed
     February 21, 2022, sites.lsa.umich.edu/inclusive-teaching/
     social-identity-wheel/.

12   DeDe Wilburn Church, "3 Micro-Messages, Their Impact, and Why
     This Matters," LinkedIn Pulse, February 28, 2019, linkedin
     .com/pulse/3-micro-messages-past-4-days-dede-wilburn-church/
     ?articleId=6506931939524509696.

CHAPTER 4

1   Michael Jr., "[#5] Amazing Grace: Break Time; Michael Jr.," YouTube
     video, 4:37, August 12, 2015, youtube.com/watch?v=oVSTKpJBq-8.

2   Dictionary.com, s.v. "ego (n.)," accessed April 21, 2022, dictionary
     .com/browse/ego.

3   "What Percentage of Our Lives Are Spent Working?," Reference, last
     updated March 24, 2020, reference.com/world-view/percentage
     -lives-spent-working-599e3f7fb2c88fca.

4   Robert I. Sutton, *Good Boss, Bad Boss: How to Be the Best . . .
     and Learn from the Worst* (New York: Grand Central Publishing,
     2019), 72.

5   Sutton, *Good Boss, Bad Boss.*

6   Sutton, *Good Boss, Bad Boss.*

7   Laurie Bennett, "Creativity, Purpose and Vulnerability," ART
     + Marketing, September 19, 2017, artplusmarketing.com/
     creativity-purpose-and-vulnerability-297fe699905c.

8   Bennett, "Creativity, Purpose and Vulnerability."

9   Trynia Kaufman, "Building Positive Relationships with Students:
     What Brain Science Says," Understood, accessed December 16,
     2020, understood.org/en/articles/brain-science-says-4-reasons-to
     -build-positive-relationships-with-students.

CHAPTER 5

1   Dictionary.com, s.v. "authentic (adj.)," accessed April 21, 2022,
     dictionary.com/browse/authentic.

2   Brené Brown, "Shame vs. Guilt," *Brené Brown* (blog), January 15, 2013, brenebrown.com/blog/2013/01/14/shame-v-guilt/.

3   Brown, "Shame vs. Guilt."

4   "Authenticity and Gen Z: Beyond the Buzzword," *Student Beans* (blog), October 19, 2021, partner.studentbeans.com/blog/gen-z -trends/gen-z-authenticity/.

5   "Authenticity," *Psychology Today*, accessed February 21, 2022, psychologytoday.com/us/basics/authenticity.

6   Hot News Daily, "'Jiggly Boy' Returns . . . and KG Approves: Funny Video 2015," YouTube video, March 1, 2015, youtube.com/ watch?v=0SfVJS39Cuo.

7   Brené Brown, *The Gifts of Imperfection* (New York: Random House, 2020), 6.

8   Tim Walker, "Survey: Alarming Number of Educators May Soon Leave the Profession," National Education Association, February 1, 2022, nea.org/advocating-for-change/new-from-nea/survey -alarming-number-educators-may-soon-leave-profession.

9   Brené Brown, *The Gifts of Imperfection* (New York: Random House, 2020).

10 Tchiki Davis, "What Is Self-Awareness, and How Do You Get It?," *Psychology Today* (blog), March 11, 2019, psychologytoday.com/us/ blog/click-here-happiness/201903/what-is-self-awareness-and-how -do-you-get-it.

11 Tchiki Davis, "What Is Self-Awareness?"

12 "Authenticity," *Psychology Today*, accessed February 21, 2022, psychologytoday.com/us/basics/authenticity.

13 Gary Keller and Jay Papasan, *The One Thing: The Surprisingly Simple Truth behind Extraordinary Results* (London: John Murray Press, 2019), 1444.

14 Shawn Achor, *The Orange Frog: A Parable Based on Positive Psychology* (Apex, NC: International Thought Leader Network, 2013).

15 "Character Strengths," VIA Institute on Character, accessed April 21, 2022, viacharacter.org/character-strengths-via.

16 Brené Brown, *The Gifts of Imperfection* (New York: Random House, 2020), 157.

CHAPTER 6

1   Dave Davies, "Meet the 7 Most Popular Search Engines in the World," *Search Engine Journal*, March 3, 2021, searchenginejournal .com/seo-101/meet-search-engines/.

2   Kathleen Cushman, "What Does a Critical Friends Group Do?," Coalition of Essential Schools, February 11, 1997, essentialschools .org/horace-issues/what-does-a-critical-friends-group-do/.

3   Christiane Fellbaum (1998, ed.) WordNet: An Electronic Lexical Database. Cambridge, MA: MIT Press.

4   *Cambridge Dictionary*, s.v. "willingness (n.)," accessed April 21, 2022, dictionary.cambridge.org/us/dictionary/english/willingness.

5   Definitions.net, "willingness," July 9, 2019, definitions.net/definition/ willingness.

6   Oliver Wendell Holmes Jr., "One's mind, Once Stretched by a New Idea, Never Regains Its Original Dimensions," Quotes.net, accessed April 21, 2022, quotes.net/quote/4003.

7   Libby Simon, "How Information Overload Affects the Brain," Psych Central, March 15, 2018, psychcentral.com/pro/how-information -overload-affects-the-brain.

8   John C. Maxwell, *The 21 Indispensable Qualities of a Leader: Becoming the Person Others Will Want to Follow* (Nashville: Thomas Nelson, 2012).

CONCLUSION

1   George Couros, *The Innovator's Mindset (The Podcast)*, accessed April 21, 2022, podcasts.apple.com/us/podcast/the -innovators-mindset-the-podcast/id1155968930.

ACKNOWLEDGMENTS

First and foremost, I thank God for the many blessings and opportunities He's allowed me to experience, specifically the people He's allowed me to meet.

I would like to thank my wife, Samantha, and daughter, Gabrielle, for supporting this work and being my most important cheerleaders. Without their unconditional love, encouragement, and constructive criticism, I would still be wondering *what if* instead of relishing what we accomplished. Samantha and Gabrielle are my inspiration.

I would like to thank my mother, Charmel Carter, my big sister, Nicole Burton, my twin brother, Dwayne Carter, and my extended family. My mother has sacrificed so much to enable my siblings and me to excel. My success is a direct reflection of her love, correction, and vision for my life. My sister Nicki's creative style and entrepreneurial spirit inspire me every day to free myself from the mental traps I set. My twin brother, Dwayne, continues to inspire me with his genuine love, support, and encouragement. My success is our family's success!

I'm thankful to the staff at IMPress for their patience, unconditional support, accountability, and guidance. They have believed in me and my work for many years. I am forever grateful for their friendship.

I would especially like to thank my educator friends who shared their stories in this book. I am so thankful for my friend and confidant George Couros for constantly pushing me to excel as an educator and leader, inspiring me to think differently about education, and putting my thoughts and reflections into words.

ABOUT THE AUTHOR

Dwight L. Carter is a nationally recognized school leader, speaker, and presenter from Columbus, Ohio. He has been a teacher, athletic coach, assistant principal, and principal. Because of his collaborative and innovative leadership, in 2010, he was inducted into the Jostens Renaissance Educator Hall of Fame. He was also named a 2013 National Association of Secondary School Principals  Digital Principal of the Year, the 2014 Academy of Arts and Science Education High School Principal of the Year, the 2015 Ohio Alliance of Black School Educators Principal of the Year, and a 2021 Columbus Africentric Early College Sankofa Emerging Leader award winner. He is currently the director of student support systems for Eastland-Fairfield Career & Technical Schools.

He is the coauthor of *What's in Your Space? 5 Steps for Better School and Classroom Design* (Corwin, 2016) and *Leading Schools in Disruptive Times: How to Survive Hyper-Change* (Corwin, 2017; second edition, 2021). He is a contributing author to *Because of a Teacher: Stories of the Past to Inspire the Future of Education* (IMPress, 2021), curated by George Couros. Additionally, he has contributed to several educational books and articles. You can connect with Dwight through Twitter (@Dwight_Carter) or his blog, *Mr. Carter's Office* (dwightcarter.edublogs.org).

MORE FROM

IMPRESS

ImpressBooks.org

Empower
What Happens when Students Own Their Learning
by A.J. Juliani and John Spencer

Learner-Centered Innovation
Spark Curiosity, Ignite Passion, and Unleash Genius
by Katie Martin

Unleash Talent
Bringing Out the Best in Yourself and the Learners You Serve
by Kara Knollmeyer

Reclaiming Our Calling
Hold On to the Heart, Mind, and Hope of Education
by Brad Gustafson

Take the L.E.A.P.
Ignite a Culture of Innovation
by Elisabeth Bostwick

Drawn to Teach
An Illustrated Guide to Transforming Your Teaching
written by Josh Stumpenhorst and illustrated by Trevor Guthke

Math Recess
Playful Learning in an Age of Disruption
by Sunil Singh and Dr. Christopher Brownell

Innovate inside the Box
Empowering Learners Through UDL and Innovator's Mindset
by George Couros and Katie Novak

Personal & Authentic
Designing Learning Experiences That Last a Lifetime
by Thomas C. Murray

Learner-Centered Leadership
A Blueprint for Transformational Change in Learning Communities
by Devin Vodicka

Kids These Days
A Game Plan for (Re)Connecting with Those We Teach, Lead & Love
by Dr. Jody Carrington

UDL and Blended Learning
Thriving in Flexible Learning Landscapes
by Katie Novak and Catlin Tucker

Teachers These Days
Stories & Strategies for Reconnection
by Dr. Jody Carrington and Laurie McIntosh

Because of a Teacher
Stories of the Past to Inspire the Future of Education
written and curated by George Couros

Because of a Teacher, Volume II
Stories from the First Years of Teaching
written and curated by George Couros

Evolving Education
Shifting to a Learner-Centered Paradigm
by Katie Martin

Adaptable
How to Create an Adaptable Curriculum and Flexible Learning Experiences That Work in Any Environment
by A.J. Juliani

Lead from Where You Are
Building Intention, Connection, and Direction in Our Schools
by Joe Sanfelippo

Evolving with Gratitude
Small Practices in Learning Communities That Make a Big Difference with Kids, Peers, and the World
by Lainie Rowell